Praise for A Woman Unto Herself

"If ever a book could heal the heart's deepest wounds, this is it! Step by step, Ms. Benson shows us how to move through the depths of the most painful dark nights of the soul to find the kind of profound and powerful love every human being hungers for and rarely ever finds. We readily relate to her raw, honest vulnerability, as she leads us through her own personal unbearable sadness only to discover that the rich, sustaining, spiritual love she yearned for was within her own heart. Many fairy-tale love stories perpetuate the myth that someone out there will "complete" us. Ms. Benson shows us how to respond to the real world. Her hard-earned wisdom serves as a road-map for us all to find the lasting love and "wholeness" we seek. *A Woman Unto Herself* is a must-read for anyone longing for inner balance, joy, peace and most of all, true enduring love."

—Martha Borst,
bestselling author of *Your Survival Strategies Are Killing You!*

"Tina Benson's *A Woman Unto Herself* is a *game changer.* Through riveting stories of her own harrowing travels through love's labyrinths, she expertly guides readers directly to the *source of love.* In these times, when movies and fairy tales lead us down the garden path to disappointment and heartache, *A Woman Unto Herself* is a *must read.*"

—Marcia Wieder, CEO,
Dream University,
bestselling author, *Making Your Dreams Come True*

"Tina's book whispers, cries, and sings a crucial message for modern women and men: Our darkness is as important on the spiritual journey as our light. Our wounds become our flowers. This is not only fine spiritual autobiography, but essential healing."

—Alfred K. LaMotte,
author of *Wounded Bud: Poems for Meditation*

"Any man or woman who has suffered in a relationship, lost a sense of self by trying to make a bad one work, or stayed too long because of self-blame, will find a soul-sister in Tina Benson as she recounts her inspiring journey in search of true and divine self-love. From the deepest parts of her soul, she finds pearls of wisdom and shares them in the pages of *A Woman Unto Herself*—showing us that the path to wholeness and a peaceful heart resides, eternally, within oneself."

—Lily Kaplan, founder, Resh Foundation;
author, *Two Rare Birds: A Legacy of Love*

"Author and spiritual teacher, Tina Benson's *A Woman Unto Herself* does what no other memoir does: She blends 30 years of her own spiritual journey with her training in psychology, and doing so, she tells a very different kind of love story. Her raw, honest, and vulnerable self-revelations document her arduous journey toward the inner Beloved. The result: a love story that defies the cultural myths of our times, and creates a new myth for anyone looking for real, true, and sustaining love. Anyone on a spiritual journey, or anyone looking for love, will find comfort and guidance in these pages, pointing readers toward the greatest love of all. This truly is a tale with a "happy ending." Let this book surprise you . . . rip your heart open . . . challenge you . . . and guide you home."

—Marguerite Rigoglioso, Ph.D.,
Founding Director of Seven Sisters Mystery School; author of *The Cult of Divine Birth in Ancient Greece,* and *Virgin Mother Goddesses of Antiquity*

"In her spiritual autobiography, Tina Benson tells the story of many people of her generation, growing up largely detached from the Judeo-Christian tradition of earlier years, yet longing for deeper spiritual currents than modern secular rationalism can provide. Turning to the East—especially India, Hinduism and Buddhism—as well as Carl Jung's depth psychology, Benson finds deeper meaning in her search for the Divine within her own heart and consciousness. Her personal journey is a compelling story of struggle with the anomie of modern life. *A Woman Unto Herself* offers a particularly illuminating account of one woman grappling with her dysfunctional family and its impact on her life as she comes to understand, accept, forgive, and love them and herself."

—Frederick Glaysher,
poet and author of *The Parliament of Poets*

"A question often faced by both men and women: How do we deal with betrayal and grief at the loss of a closely held illusion? Tina Benson's **A Woman Unto Herself** brings up questions about "spiritual fidelity" as well as "emotional fidelity." Her description of a "loving divorce ritual" impressed me—if only they were all like that! More so, though, I am impressed with her courage to be so open and vulnerable in this book. We realize: "Here is a woman trained in psychotherapy who is just as human as the rest of us." She feels and expresses her anger, her love, her denial, and her confusion—all of which lead her (and us) toward wholeness."

—**Art Noble**,
author of *The Sacred Female,* and
Unmailed Letters to a Married Woman

A Woman Unto Herself

A Woman Unto Herself

A Different Kind of Love Story

Tina M. Benson M.A.

Disclaimer:
I have tried to recreate events, locales and conversations from my
memories of them. In order to maintain their anonymity, in some instances
I have changed the names of individuals and places. I may have changed
some identifying characteristics and details such as physical properties,
occupation and places of residence.

Cover photography by:
Santosh Kumar Pandey
http://www.flickr.com/photos/57500213@N02/
saanto_sakumar@yahoo.co.in

ISBN: 0692478787
ISBN 13: 9780692478783
Library of Congress Control Number: 2015910316
Satya Books, Mill Valley, CA

For Josh and Maya
May the Inner Beloved always guide your way home…

Table of Contents

Forward

ROMANTIC LOVE AS a spiritual pathway, in its myriad manifestations, is well-known throughout literature and art. Whether in the devotional-mystical poetry of Rumi, the couple's paths of erotic *tantra* and Taoist *neidan*, the *Old Testament "Song of Solomon"* or in the greatest love-stories of all times, love comes (hopefully!) to prevail over cynicism, strife, loneliness, and perhaps even death, as in Edgar Allan Poe's supernatural, *Annabel Lee*.

Less known, and most certainly less written about in contemporary western literature, are the mysterious passions of the "Inner Marriage" known by solo mystics of all times. In *A Woman Unto Herself: A Different Kind of Love Story*, Tina Benson describes her own very personal journey towards this sacred inner marriage.

From an early childhood inexplicably infused with experiences of The Great Mystery, through early abandonment and loss, to a 23-year sustained, creative marriage and heart-expanding motherhood, through a bittersweet divorce -- bittersweet because this particular parting of ways is so unusually filled with caring and mutual respect -- to spiritual awakenings and pilgrimages, the aftermath of a devastating romantic betrayal, and a surprising crescendo, we feel, "Yes, The Great Mystery is actually unfolding in her life."

> *"I was suddenly enveloped in a feeling of immense, universal, radiant, and unconditional love...a feeling of such an overwhelming sense of rapture, awe, wonder, and beauty it was almost unbearable to behold.*
>
> *I felt all the invisible boundaries separating me from the Divine melt away, and I knew I was part of something much greater than what my ordinary senses reveal.*
>
> *The realization remains with me today, as clear as ever: We are all one, all individual expressions of one unconditionally loving presence, the Source of everything and everyone, including me.*
>
> *I also undeniably knew that this was reality, and the rest of what I had experienced until then was illusion, what the Hindus call 'Maya.' I knew with certainty that this experience was always present and available. Like a flowing river, I just needed to step into it.*

Many Gnostic and other spiritual texts describe such transformative moments as spontaneous numinous experiences.

For this non-practicing Jew, it was as if I had had a direct experience of being bathed in 'Christ consciousness' and unconditional love. The fact that it was Easter Sunday, the day of Jesus' resurrection in the Garden, didn't escape me."

Tantric texts throughout the millenniums written by those steeped in this Great Love are said to be permeated by the catalytic energy of their author's awakenings, known as *samdhyabhasa*, "twilight communications." Readers of such texts have always been counseled to merely hold the book in one's hands in order to receive the twilight transmission of the author's awakening.

May all who read *A Woman Unto Herself: A Different Kind of Love Story* be so moved by Tina's story that merely holding her book will convey a *samdhyabhasa* transmission of awakening to truly unendable creative love.

Stuart Sovatsky, PhD
Author, *Advanced Spiritual Intimacy:
The Yoga of Deep Tantric Sensuality,
Words From the Soul: Time, East/West Spirituality and
Psychotherapeutic Narrative,* and *Your Perfect Lips:
A Spiritual-Erotic Memoir*

He came to me, finally, the lover I had longed for all my life,
And he held my face in his palms and told me I was beautiful.

And he made love to my body, knowing and cherishing my
every longing and desire;

He saw the depths of my soul and was bewildered by my beauty.

He treasured every feeling I had, licked the tears from my face,
traced my lips with his fingers, and held me in the profound
comfort of his embrace.

He anointed me in oils, bathed me, combed my hair, and of-
fered his undying devotion and worship at my feet.

He covered me in rose petals and vowed to love me forevermore.

He told me he had longed for me with as much aching in his
soul as I had longed for him.

And here, right in the center of my own heart, I found him . . .
The very last place I had thought to look.

My Personal Message To You...

LOVE AND LONGING have been constant companions of mine ever since my first numinous, transcendent experience at age seven. From then on, I have felt the presence of an infinite source of unconditional love, of which I am a part, and I have *longed* to remember that truth in my bones, and to live it daily. Fueled by desire, my early spiritual experience sent my soul on a journey . . . to understand the experience . . . to feel and embody it . . . and to light a path in the darkness for others to follow.

Many religious and spiritual traditions warn us of the dangers of longing and desire, believing them to be the root of all suffering. According to such teachings, we should aim to rid ourselves of all desires in order to be spiritually free.

However, other spiritual traditions (often esoteric branches of mainstream religions) have, throughout time, sought to use longing and desire as effective pathways to God. For example, in Hinduism, spiritual seekers can follow the *bhakti* path—cultivating experiences of love, devotion, and embracing the desire for union with the divine. Hindus use music, chanting, poetry, and dance to fan the flames of longing for the divine beloved. Sufis achieve this through dervish dances, whirling and spinning to open up to God's presence. Mystic poets—such as Kabir, Rumi, and Hafiz—have gifted the world with beautiful poems of longing and love for the divine.

Whether through dance, music, poetry, chanting, or ecstatic trance states, these practices aim to help spiritual aspirants to *lean into longing.* In these traditions, longing is seen, not as the cause of all suffering, but as a path to transcendence and union with God (Source/Spirit/the Divine Beloved).

Longing has always been my muse: I followed the *bhakti* path long before I knew the term. From that first numinous experience at seven—to every lover who aroused a deep longing in me for union, intimacy, and transcendence, to my deepest longing for union with God, surrendering to the Mystery—longing has always been my guide. At every turn, I have sought to bear the fire of my longing, to breathe onto its embers and listen to the sometimes faint whispers of my own longing in order to find my way when I have felt lost and confused.

While I have spent time meditating and entering transcendent states, in caves and temples with holy men in the Himalayas as well as in more mundane places (such as on my meditation pillow in my living room), I can access the Mystery in many ways—through profound silence and solitude, walking in nature, going all the way into and through anguish, sorrow, loss, or heartbreak, and via lovemaking where I open the portals at the top of my womb to lift both myself and my lover directly up and into the ecstatic realms of spirit. Perhaps because I had my first numinous experience spontaneously at seven, the Mystery is never really all that far away from me.

Despite what some psycho-spiritual traditions teach, desire has not been a source of suffering for me. In fact, it has been a path to my salvation, leading me evermore toward the deepest truths of my soul, pointing me in the direction of my greatest hopes and dreams, and giving me fortitude in the midst of doubt, despair, and uncertainty. Longing itself has been much like a beloved. I have listened to its whispers in the middle of the night, giving me the courage to be my most vulnerable, naked, and undisguised self, and to hold my desires as sacred expressions from my soul.

I have longed for love, for spiritual communion, and also for particular places. My soul whispers to me that my spiritual home lies in India. My longing has always been the altar at which I pray, and, even now, all I can do in the face of its desires is to humbly, and with profound gratitude, bow and pray, in yearning and surrender.

This book is the raw and exposed story of my personal journey from longing to love—all of the ways I looked for it in all the wrong places, and how, finally, I found my way to an enduring love deep inside my own heart. Having been married for twenty-three years, and having taught couples workshops and retreats, and counseled couples for decades, I had always imagined my book would show people how to cultivate nourishing outer relationships. However, now that it's written, I am surprised to see how my book turned out to be more an intimate telling of my own personal journey—from longing and loss to the ultimate discovery of my own ever-present inner Beloved.

I wrote *A Woman Unto Herself* mainly to document my journey from a search for love in someone "out there" to a slow turning inward to find the source and satisfaction of a beloved/sacred marriage within my own being. I hope to inspire others, men and women, to likewise turn inward toward their own inner beloved—not to the exclusion of, but in addition to, the love of an outer beloved.

Through the visual imagery of the written word, I have attempted to convey what I mean by a sacred, sexual, reverential, and devotional connection with an outer lover. In sharing my story, I hope to give readers permission to claim their own sexual and spiritual desires and appetites, and to highlight the difference between feeling "exposed" and vulnerable and being "embarrassed," which implies some degree of shame. I have no shame about my sexuality or my desires and I hope that my story, and my courage to tell it, gives others permission to celebrate their own sacred sexuality.

I expect readers will react to my story in a variety of ways—particularly to passages that deal explicitly with sex and intimacy. In fact, some readers might feel embarrassed *for me*—thinking I have gone too far . . . *exposed too much.* While writing this book, I made peace with the fact that I can't know, much less control, how my readers will think, feel, or react to what I've written.

I offer my words and insights with humility and profound gratitude for everything that has happened to me in my life so far—the heartbreaks and the breakthroughs—and, from the bottom of my heart, I thank everyone who has been a part of my journey; who has helped me, hurt me, guided me, confused me, loved me, tormented me, saved me, abandoned me, believed in me, denigrated me, held me, dropped me, betrayed me and nourished me . . . all have been great and profound teachers, and I bow in deep gratitude to all of you.

Sharing my story, I trust, will offer comfort, guidance, companionship, hope, encouragement, inspiration, and faith as you walk the unpredictable, often painful, confusing, and joyful journey of your own life. My prayer for you, as it has always been for myself, is that you come to know you are deeply loved—in fact, that *you are love itself. Namaste.*

Tina Benson
Stinson Beach, California
August 30th

Part 1
Betrayal

Prologue

THREE-AND-A-HALF YEARS AFTER we met, Pritam and I traveled together to Costa Rica for our "moonhoney"—to celebrate the renewal of our love, following an emotionally difficult year. My fiftieth birthday was coming up, so I had rented an exquisite private villa for a two-week getaway in Manuel Antonio, on the Pacific coast.

During the second week, Pritam would fly back to England for his summer teaching schedule as a linguistics professor at the University of Cambridge, and I would spend the rest of my time in Costa Rica with five of my best girlfriends and their daughters, along with my own daughter, Maya, my cousin, and my eldest sister—a women's retreat to honor my birthday and to help usher me across the threshold into my new decade.

As anticipated, the first week with my sweetheart turned out to be a passionate, love-filled, sexual adventure. We went horseback riding along a creek deep in the rainforest, hiked through the national park admiring exotic local wildlife, spent a day on a catamaran with whales all around us, and watched a pair of turtles during their mating ritual. We took a boat ride through the mangroves, and fed bananas to capuchin monkeys right out of our hands. We ate delicious local foods, lovingly cooked by the villa staff. We dined in candlelight watching the sun set over the Pacific, and enjoyed the spectacle of sunrise from the luxury of a hot tub. We made passionate, wild and crazy love, endlessly, until deliriously satiated. When the time came for Pritam to leave, ending our glorious adventure, I kissed him in the early morning light as the taxi waited to take him to the airport, knowing I would have to wait two months before I would see him again.

I spent the next twenty-four hours alone, before my "women's cohort" arrived, indulging myself in a full-day spa, just up the road from the villa. The good times continued with family and friends, lots of great food, frequent bouts of laughing, sharing, dancing, more spa treatments, and excursions into the exotic bounty that Costa Rica offers—from a full day zip-lining in the rainforest to shopping in the small neighboring town of Quepos. I felt honored throughout this special time, surrounded by the love of the most important women in my life—women who have held me up when I felt down or lost; who reminded me of my courage when I felt afraid; who believed in me, stood by me, supported me, and loved me no matter what, no matter when, no questions asked.

For my birthday ritual, I had invited the women to gather in a circle inspired by Native American councils. I wanted to ask them a specific question, going around the circle using a talking stick, each offering her thoughts, wisdom, and feminine "knowing." At the appropriate time, we sat together according to age, from youngest to oldest. As it happened, we spanned exactly fifty-years—from my ten-year old daughter to my older sister aged sixty.

Once settled in, I asked my assembled tribe: "*What does it mean to be a 'woman unto oneself'?*" This question had become a kind of prayer for me the closer I got to fifty. But what exactly did it mean? Following the ancient tradition of sacred tribal council, each woman offered her heartfelt response into the circle.

Their collective wisdom exceeded my expectations—a truly sacred process. Each woman drew on her own lived experience. They spoke of honoring their own needs and wants, while also honoring those of others. Many expressed a desire for solitude, more time to tend to their own souls. A common theme emerged: Each woman needed to feel whole unto herself—to gratify her own passions, whims, and fancies, and to spend less time just taking care of others.

The older women talked about the importance of trusting their own intuition, and the teenage girls cried with gratitude to be in the presence of their elders. We all laughed and cried, and from each other's life stories we learned what it means to become a "woman unto herself." Maya, my ten-year-old, summed up our shared wisdom: "If you feel 'yes,' say, 'yes'; and if you feel 'no,' say 'no.'" How much easier all our lives might have been had we lived with that simple clarity all along! I will always be grateful to my "council of feminine wisdom" for their heartfelt generosity and grace and for carrying me across the threshold into my fifties.

In return, I gifted each woman with a small Costa Rican handmade wooden bowl, inscribed with a word that captured, for me, her essence: "Seeker," "Wisdom," "Faith," "Truth," "Loyalty," "Courage," "Family," "Beauty," "Kindness," "Sweetness," and "Love."

I returned home overflowing with love and gratitude, eager and ready to celebrate my upcoming actual birthday. I had rented a charming little house right on the beach for ten days, intending to *finally* start writing the book that had been burning in my soul for years. At last, I felt prepared and confident enough to tell my story.

Those glorious ten days at the beach house nourished my soul even more, building on the care and friendship I had received in Costa Rica. On top of all that, I was madly in love with a man in England, who would return to me in a few months. With this cocktail of experiences tingling through my veins, I blissfully dived into writing. Page after page effortlessly poured out of me. I had never been this happy in my life.

CHAPTER 1

Ecstasy to Agony

IN THE BLINK of an eye, my entire world came crashing down. Suddenly and unexpectedly, my life and all my dreams shattered into a million pieces.

It all began innocently enough one Friday morning as I walked into my office for a full day with clients. At that very moment, my Indian sweetheart, Pritam, was on a plane from England to Los Angeles, to be with me for a five-day lovefest in San Francisco before flying back to England to teach linguistics at Cambridge University for the Fall semester. We both eagerly anticipated our reunion, emailing and texting each other multiple times a day.

I hardly ever receive mail at my office, so I've no idea what compelled me to check the mailbox that morning. I was surprised to find two envelopes typewritten and addressed to me, both postmarked from England, without any return address. I imagined Pritam had sent me love letters to arrive before his flight. With mounting excitement, I opened the envelopes and had just started reading the first letter when my client arrived on schedule. The typewritten words jumped off the page and struck me like a hot knife:

"Your man is not faithful to you. He will deny it very skillfully and make up stories very artfully, but it is true. Why is the woman the last to know? Why doesn't someone tell her the truth? You would be wise to listen to your gut instincts Tina, to practice safe sex whenever he comes back from his travels, and to protect your assets from this moment onwards. You would be wise to ask yourself, 'What do you truly know about his other lives, his past, his worlds overseas?' As a Jungian, you should trust your inner knowing more and awaken to the archetype that is being represented in this situation."

Along with the note, the envelope contained a photocopied article on "Lying In Relationships" and another on "Narcissism."

Stunned, shaken, and confused, I tried to gather myself to be fully present for my client. For some mysterious reason, as he sat down on the couch he said:

"I was thinking about you the other day and how many people you have helped. I just want you to know I said a prayer for you that nothing bad should ever happen to you."

He had never said anything remotely like that to me before, and I have no idea why he spoke those words that morning. It took all I had to muster an appropriate therapeutic response. I managed to choke out something along the lines of:

"Thank you. I take that as an expression of appreciation and gratitude for the work we have done together."

Behind my professional facade, I was tumbling off the edge of a cliff I hadn't even known was there. Somehow, through the grace of God, and from years working as a coach, I managed to pry my awareness back to my client—fully present for him, his life, his struggles, his sorrows—as I did for the rest of my clients that day.

By lunchtime, I had managed to convince myself that the letters were sent by some spurned woman whose advances or admiration Pritam had rebuffed, and that she had sent those shocking letters as a form of revenge. Of course, given my profession, I should have known better: The mind's capacity for denial—in particular, *my* capacity for denial—about the actions of a loved one knew no bounds (more on this later). I knew Pritam would have landed in L.A. by then, so I texted him:

"I have a break for lunch, please call." He didn't. I told myself he was probably exhausted from the long flight and napping. I texted him again at 5:30, after my last client:

"I really need to talk with you, how late can I call?"

"What's up?" he finally responded.

I texted back: "I can't really get into it right now, I'm just leaving to meet some friends for dinner. How late can I call you?"

He dialed me immediately to find out what was wrong.

"I really don't think now would be a good time to get into this, I'm on my way to dinner.

"*What's up?!*" This time he was more forceful and insistent.

"Well, I walked into my office this morning to find two envelopes waiting for me postmarked from England." I read out the damning paragraph.

"Do you have any idea who would have sent this to me and why?" His silence spoke volumes.

"Have you been having an affair?" More deafening silence. "Well, that's an easy question for an innocent man to answer. I guess there's something you need to tell me . . . *I am on my way to dinner and can't get into this right now. Call me later tonight.*"

I hung up, went to dinner with my friends, and, because everything in me fought to disbelieve the unfolding horror, I said nothing to them. Naively, I hoped some good explanation would emerge to dissolve this nightmare.

Somehow, I managed to get through the meal without totally falling apart, and went home to wait for his call—it never came.

The next morning, he finally phoned. Under normal circumstances, I would pick him up at Oakland airport, wrap my arms around him, whisper how much I loved and missed him, and then both of us would return to the home we had shared for three years, and make passionate love for five days before he left for Cambridge. But that all changed the moment the phone rang.

CHAPTER 2

- ❦ -

Warning Signs

OUR RELATIONSHIP HAD been tumultuous from the start. We first met in India at a professional conference on psychology and spirituality, where we both gave talks. I was sitting in the audience for a presentation and panel discussion on "What Happens At The Moment Of Death." Just a few months before, I had held my best friend's eight-year old daughter in my arms as she died, and I was eager to hear what the panel had to say. At the end of the presentation, the discussion opened up for a Q&A session, and I shared my experience of holding Morgan as she passed away. The Indian man who would become my lover and partner sat several rows behind me in the huge auditorium. He sought me out during the next break as I stood in line for a cup of tea.

"I heard what you had to say about holding your friend's dying daughter, and was very moved," he said. "I had a similar experience when my wife died. Can we talk?"

"Sure," I said, and we found a table.

As we talked, I sensed how much this man loved his wife who had died of cancer six years before, and that he still deeply grieved her loss. As we exchanged business cards, I said, "If you are ever in California please contact me. It would be lovely to have tea or share a meal together." I had just ended my own marriage after twenty-three years, and wasn't looking for, or thinking about, this man as a potential future partner. His obvious love for his deceased wife touched me, and I offered to send him a copy of a short film I had made on "Love."

After the conference, I took a group of people touring through India, and when I returned to the U.S., I sent him the DVD as I had promised. I never heard back from him and didn't think twice about it. My ex-husband and I were in the middle of selling our home, and I was resettling into a new life with my young daughter as a single mother.

Six months later, I received an email saying he would be in the States on a business trip, so we arranged to meet for breakfast. Our conversation went deep and we lost track of time, until the staff began clearing away the dishes. He told me he was trying to extricate himself from a relationship back in England. Before we left the restaurant, he slipped a small tape recorder across the table to me, along with a set of earbuds, and asked me to listen to a recording of a channeling session he had had with a psychic. I listened as she predicted he would soon be living in the U.S. Back at my car, he kissed me gently, and my body said "yes."

He left on a road trip to L.A. for a family wedding. "What a lovely man," I thought. "If I'm ever in England, I'll look him up." He had asked me to order a book for him he couldn't find in England, and that launched us into what became a long-distance love affair for three months, through emails, text messages, and phone calls.

As we got to know each other, we gradually fell in love, writing poetry back and forth, sharing intimacies, dreams, hopes, longings, desires. Three months later, when he returned to the States for a week's visit, I was already well on my way to being in love. He was (and no doubt still is) a brilliant, charismatic, interesting, complex, passionate man. I had left my marriage after so many years mainly because I longed for a deeper sexual, spiritual, and emotional connection, and despite years of couples therapy and even Tantra workshops together, my husband and I did not have any sexual chemistry—we never had. But this man and I had boundless sexual and spiritual chemistry. Making love with him felt transcendent—finally, I could feel a long-dormant part of me joyfully and blissfully coming alive again.

Before he arrived, I had transformed my bed into an altar, a sacred space, covered it with rose petals, and made a ritualized offering of flowers, incense, rose water, frankincense, and myrrh. And so, I prepared for our first sexual greeting. Although we had fallen in love over emails, text messages, and phone calls, I had yet to know how our bodies would respond to each other. I remember exhaling a deep sigh of relief when everything in my body said, "Yes, yes, yes!" We spent a glorious week discovering each other sexually, making love all day and night, taking walks to the ocean, cooking together, falling more and more deeply in love. At the end of the week, he went back East for a professional conference, and then returned to England.

We made plans to meet in Barcelona two months later, after a conference where I gave a talk. We rented a flat just across the street from the Mediterranean, spent most days making love until mid-afternoon, and then leisurely strolled through the streets of Barcelona, exploring its beauty and mystery, sampling delicious Spanish food and wine, delighting in the extraordinary architecture, and visiting superb art museums, topped off every evening with romantic dinners— truly, a lover's paradise. I had never been happier and more in love, sharing the unique sights, sounds, and aromas of this magnificent city with a man I was crazy about.

After our love-drenched week together, he headed back to England and I returned to the States. We made plans for me to visit him at his vacation home in India a month later. Despite the daunting distance between us, I figured if we could manage to see each other every two or three months, our relationship could work. To help things along, he arranged to teach at Stanford every six months; and within a year we had set up home together, living half the year in California, and traveling together to England or India for at least another month during the other half of the year. We also managed to squeeze in shorter visits when he would come to the States for professional conferences.

That December, six months after our love affair had begun, and just a month after our trip to Barcelona, I visited him in India. I saw unmistakable warning signs of the tragedies to come, but ignored them. Instead, I distorted the reality in front of me, just as I had learned to do as a child with my father.

Warning Signs

Pritam and his late wife had purchased a home in Puttaparthi, a small town outside Bangalore developed around the world-renowned guru Sattya Sai Baba. His family, his wife in particular, were ardent devotees, although he claimed not to be a devotee of anyone or anything, and took great pride in his philosophical nihilism. Nevertheless, he traveled to Puttaparthi every year around the holidays for spiritual rest and rejuvenation, and made daily pilgrimages to Sai Baba's ashram.

Within a day of my arrival, I realized I had not brought appropriate ashram attire, so I went into town to buy a few sets of *salwar kameez*—the pants and long tunic-like blouses worn by the women of India. Warning sign number one: Gone less than two hours, I returned to proudly show him my bargains (haggling is an expected form of commercial discourse in most "third-world" cultures). Rather than celebrate my trove, Pritam accused me of having affairs in the back of the shop with the Kashmiri traders. Nothing I said could dissuade him from his suspicions and paranoia. His reaction stunned me. In vain, I protested my innocence, but he wouldn't listen, opening a huge rift between us.

The rest of the trip proved equally difficult. Temperamental, moody, hostile, verbally aggressive, distrustful, suspicious, and angry . . . this was not the man I thought I knew and had fallen in love with. I could not understand how this man—who had been so loving and caring during our time together in my home, in his many emails to me, and especially during our "paradise" visit to Barcelona—could be such a different person. Faced with a clear case of Dr. Jekkyl and

Mr. Hyde, I had no idea what to do or whom I was dealing with. Furthermore, I felt trapped in his home, in a foreign country. I thought about leaving and flying back early. Instead, I did what I had learned to do in childhood: I tried harder to love him, tried harder to forgive him his bad behavior, tried harder to prove myself trustworthy, believing he would come to trust that I was who I said I was. I excused his paranoia telling myself that, because of his wife's death, he was afraid of losing me. I made excuses for him. I tried to understand his painful childhood growing up poor and impoverished, first in India and then in Fiji. He never really opened up about the details of his childhood, but I gleaned enough to understand it was painful, abusive, and traumatic. Being an understanding, empathic, compassionate person, I forgave him and dug deeper into myself to find even more empathy and compassion for his wounded heart.

It would take years, and deep excavation of my own soul, for me to realize just how big a mistake that was.

Part 2
Legacies

CHAPTER 3

❧

Motherless Daughters

I WAS BORN to a troubled mother, a jazz singer, and a narcissistic but affectionate father who was a very funny vaudevillian comedian, and a mediocre jazz drummer. My parents met in a Los Angeles jazz club in 1960. She, a gorgeous, sultry, sexy, voluptuous, and supremely talented but emotionally broken woman, bewitched my eternally horny and on-the-prowl father—and soon I was conceived. My father did the "responsible" thing by marrying her, though I doubt he had wanted the responsibilities of husband and father.

My mother, father, uncle (my father's brother), and a close friend of theirs, were traveling the Las Vegas nightclub circuit performing as a comedy/jazz group called "Three Cats & A Kitten" around the time I was born. A family joke tagged them as "tremendously famous, if only in their own minds." The truth, however, was that my father—a charming and charismatic playboy—had chosen the entertainment business because, as he told me, "It was the only business I could think of that would let me sleep in late, spend all day playing golf or football, or being on the beach." He truly had no grander ambitions, and he found a lifestyle that meagerly supported him. By the time my cousin and I were about a year old, they decided that "schlepping" two young babies around Las Vegas wasn't really working, so they "retired" from showbiz, and told us for the rest of our lives that we were to blame for the ending of their spectacular careers.

The early Sixties, of course, were an interesting time. I was a tail-end Baby Boomer, born just two years before Martin Luther King's famous "I Have A Dream" speech, just two years before John F. Kennedy was shot, seven years before his brother Robert F. Kennedy was assassinated, bringing the era of Camelot to an abrupt end. I was born just four years before Malcolm X was killed, seven years before Dr. King was murdered, eight years before Neil Armstrong and his cohorts made the first landing on the moon. It was a time of fierce civil rights protests and uprisings—nine years before the Kent State shootings, the height of the Women's Liberation Movement, and smack dab in the middle of the hippie cultural revolution of "peace, love, and rock-n-roll." The Beatles arrived in the States for the first time three years after I was born, unleashing a frenzy of bra-slinging adulation, then the Rolling Stones arrived soon after, and Bob Dylan was singing, *The Times They Are A Changing,* as if that needed to be stated.

To say my early years coincided with massive social, political, spiritual, and emotional upheaval would be a radical understatement. But I do wonder how those external social forces shaped and informed me, along with millions of others in my generation, not just in the US, but around the world. By the time I was ten, everything I have mentioned above had already happened on the global stage, though I was largely unconscious of the events and their profound significance, trying to find my own footing in the turbulence of my own private and personal story.

Before I was two-and-a-half, my mother had left. She had had an increasing and debilitating fear of being left alone with me. After the abrupt end of their show business career, my father had become a salesman for a wine distribution company, and was often away and on the road. Left alone with me, the demons of my mother's childhood came howling back, and she began to fear she would hurt me. For nine years, no one knew where she was.

My father, completely ill-equipped to deal with my emotional devastation, took the "ostrich approach," buried his head in the sand and acted as if she had never existed, hoping I would either not notice or not burden him with my blinding grief and loss.

As all children do with childhood trauma, I assessed the situation in my little two-year-old mind, and devised the best strategy I could to survive it. When my father did not mention her the morning she left, or again the next morning, or the next, I quickly figured out that my best strategy to preserve my relationship with him and hold onto the only liferaft I had in a now very frightening and unpredictable ocean, was to go along with the ruse and adopt the pretense, "What Mother?" We never mentioned her from that day forward. Sometimes, when I would fall asleep in his lap watching television, I would cry out in my sleep, "I miss my mommy"—his only clue to my suffering. We can, perhaps, fool the conscious mind, but the unconscious never forgets and is always—*always*—trying to heal us.

All children find ways to survive the unsurvivable. If some hope of getting love remains, we will contort ourselves, abandon ourselves, and lie to ourselves just to survive and get whatever love is available to us. If no hope exists—or, worse, is blocked by violence or abuse—we will shut down our hearts, reject ourselves, turn the violence inward and/or strike out at others as a way to protect ourselves from the devastating hurt. Because I had a father who was at least physically affectionate, I clung desperately to him, becoming a "daddy's girl," adoring him, feeding his narcissism, and completely suppressed the reality of my own shattering loss and grief. I effectively abandoned myself and, in doing so, embedded my childhood fear and anger deep into the structure of my personality. To some extent, I took these "wounds" with me into all my relationships, and only after years of therapy and personal growth-work was I finally able to unravel the mystery of who I am.

Somehow, my father and I managed after my mother left. We moved in with his parents, who looked after me while he worked. My family history is littered with a long lineage of motherless daughters, and I've often wondered about the sacred purpose of these characters in literature, fairytales, and mythology. Many of the childhood stories I grew up with feature motherless daughters as the heroine: Cinderella, Arielle from *The Little Mermaid,* Belle from *Beauty And The Beast,* Snow White, and so many others. According to sacred psychology, it typically works like this: Some traumatic event propels the heroine on her "hero's journey," as Joseph Campbell referred to it. Just as an irritating grain of sand rubbing against the inside of an oyster shell creates the beauty of a pearl, so the emotional irritation of childhood trauma propels us out into life to begin the hero's journey—and so it has been in my life.

My paternal grandmother was born in 1891 in a little Russian village just outside Kiev (now part of Ukraine). Though it was unusual for that time, her parents had divorced, and her father had immigrated to America, settling in Boston's Jewish community. Although my grandmother's grandfather had been a rabbi in Russia, once in the States, the family made every attempt to distance themselves from their Jewishness, particularly after Hitler condemned us as pariahs.

When she was just eleven, my grandmother was put on a Russian ship by her mother and sent across the ocean to live with her father, whom she couldn't remember, and his new family. I cannot imagine the terror, loss, and sense of abandonment she must have endured on the many lonely months of her journey at sea. She never saw or spoke to her mother again—a time long before computers, Skype, and cell phones. If her caretakers had had the benefit of modern psychological understanding, most likely my grandmother would have been offered counseling during her childhood.

She arrived in Boston after many months at sea, into a family she didn't know, never to see her mother again. In retrospect, I believe she would have been diagnosed with bipolar disorder as an adult, as my father described her emotional mood swings during his childhood as ranging from mania, when she would believe that the president of the United States was coming over to the house for dinner, to debilitating bouts of depression and suicidal threats or attempts that required periodic hospitalizations. The psyche does what it has to do to survive the unsurvivable.

Understanding my grandmother's emotional instability helped me to understand my father's inability to deal not only with mine, but with anyone else's feelings, including his own. His mother's emotions were so erratic and frightening to him as a young child that he became excessively rational and scientific as a reactive defense-survival strategy. He lifted himself up and out of the unpleasantness and dangers of his emotional world, and constructed an alternative rational world where he would be "safe." Not until my stepmother's death, when I was almost thirty-seven, did I see my father cry for the first and only time.

One day, while my father and I were out shopping at Ralph's supermarket in Los Angeles (I was four-and-a-half), my father met the woman who was to become my stepmother. Ever the ladies man, he was attracted by her "fabulous ass." He stalked her throughout the store and managed to finagle his way behind her in the checkout line, struck up a conversation, poured on the charm, and managed to get her phone number all before the clerk had rung up her groceries. She told me later that only because I was there and she could see how much he loved me, did she trust this stranger enough to give him her number.

Also from a showbiz background, Geri was a divorced mother with three kids. In the '30's, her step-father and his brothers founded the famous singing group, The Merry Macs, and they had performed live and on television with Bing Crosby as well as with other top acts of the day. She, too, had sung with The Merry Macs in the late 50's and early 60's until her divorce. Geri was a stunning, blonde, Amazon woman—a "*shiksa*" fantasy of many Jewish boys. True to form, my father fell for her hard. She, too, had been a motherless daughter for most of her childhood; her emotionally abusive mother had, on and off, put her and her brother in various orphanages throughout her childhood.

By the time I was six-and-a-half, she married my dad—creating an instant family for me: two new sisters, one nine and one ten years older than I, plus an older brother (by seven years), and *finally*, a mom. I was ecstatic. Although I tested her mercilessly for the first few years to see if she really loved me and would stay, I was desperately grateful to have a mother. In fact, she turned out to be a guardian angel, one of my emotional saviors. I am fairly certain that only because of her emotional wisdom and sensitivity I avoided taking a disastrously wrong turn somewhere along the way.

She was the first person to look at me and ask, "You had a mom and she left. What are you feeling about all of it?" She got our family into therapy, and although I don't recall it being particularly effective (I went screaming from the first session and never wanted to go back; it was all too much to feel at that young age), I knew she acknowledged my pain, "saw" me, and loved me absolutely every bit as much as her own three biological children. As is often the case, grace and serendipity brought two people together for mutual healing: Mothering me as an abandoned daughter helped her to heal her own wounds of abandonment. We became each other's healers, although we were not consciously aware of it at the time.

Not only did I grow to adore her, but I also worshipped my new three older siblings. They were gorgeous, cool, hip, hippies and I aspired to be just like them. I tagged along as often as they would tolerate me, and as adolescence dawned, I followed their example by diving into "sex, drugs, and rock-n-roll" rampant in L.A. during the revolutionary 60s and 70s. Drugs of all kinds flowed abundantly—particularly at the Hollywood homes of movie producers who would hand out Quaaludes, cocaine, and marijuana to innocent, sexually ripe young girls, then spirit us away into rooms hidden behind mirrors for anonymous or group sex. Groomed as daddy's little girl, I gave myself to countless men during my adolescence in a misguided attempt to find love and approval. Give me a "Rorer 714" pill, and I gladly spread my legs without ever having to know your name.

After my father remarried, and throughout my early childhood, I periodically asked about my birth mother and where she had gone. Nobody seemed to know what had become of her. She resurfaced when I was eleven. I subsequently discovered she had been living variously in Hawaii and Puerto Rico as a jazz singer, and her family had tracked her down via a private detective because her mother was dying. She returned to the States to be with her mother as she died, and decided then that she wanted and needed to take care of her unfinished business with me. She called the same phone number my father had had when she left us nine years earlier, and, miraculously, he answered. He and my stepmother discussed whether or not to risk introducing her back into my life and, with consultation from a psychologist, they decided that since I had been asking about her over the years, it would be a good thing to do.

I don't know how much time elapsed between her first phone call and the day of our dramatic "reunion," but I do vividly remember the scene at the airport. In all the years she had been gone, I had had only two pictures of her, both with very heavy and frightening stage make-up that made her look much like a female version of Leonard Nimoy's "Spock" in *Star Trek*. I remember picking out a special dress with my stepmom, going to the airport, waiting at the gate (pre-9/11), and seeing a woman walking off the plane who looked *exactly* like me, followed by her best friend and her stepfather.

Having learned earlier on to detach from my emotional reality, the moment was supremely surreal. I could not deny that this woman was my "mother," yet I had no emotional connection to her, no memories whatsoever of her from before she had left, and I was decidedly confused about what and how I was supposed to feel. Ever the dutiful daughter, I went along with the situation and made nice. We hugged, she cried, everyone else cried, and I smiled.

Being the saint that she was, my stepmom welcomed her into our home and into our lives. She spent every Christmas and Thanksgiving with us, and, as a result, our photo albums are filled with images of this integrated "family" with my two mothers. I spent summer vacations visiting her in New Jersey where she settled. She took me to jazz clubs where she sang, pointed me out to the crowd as her daughter, and then sang Roberta Flack's, *The First Time Ever I Saw Your Face* directly to me. If I had had a sarcastic bone in my good-girl body at that time, I'd have probably cracked wise with something along the lines of, "Yeah, you left this face after you saw it the first time—you abandoning fuck." But then those sentiments were not to surface until many years later in therapy. For the time being, I played the good daughter, yet again, became her good girl, let her show me off with pride at her jazz clubs, and endured the parade of new boyfriends each summer I went to visit. Not surprisingly, I grew further and further away from myself and my true feelings.

I don't remember much about the drug-hazed years of my adolescence—except for innumerable scenes of parties with cocaine, Quaaludes, hashish, pot, angel dust, and random sex, mostly with men, sometimes with women, and some-times in groups, and, sometimes with my friend's parents who also, on occasion, happened to be our drug supplier. The good girl was beginning to go bad.

My first encounter with the delights of sexuality hap-pened at age seven when I spontaneously discovered how *really* good it felt when I'd rub myself naked up against the seam of my mattress in bed. That mattress became my best friend for quite a long time. Years later, as a pre-adolescent,

I awkwardly experimented with kissing during games of "Truth or Dare," then the Halleluiah discovery of foreplay, which happened, oddly enough, when my parents would drop me off at church on Sunday mornings for the youth group. They had no religious motivation, just a place to put me on Sunday mornings to give them a break. Kenny and I would slip out the back, unlock his parents' car, and he would finger me. I immediately experienced this act as particularly pleasurable and exciting.

At fourteen, I decided it was time to lose my virginity and had sex unceremoniously for the first time in the backseat of a Camaro with a guy named Steve I had picked up while buying shoes with my father at Kinny's shoe store. It took years before I learned to bring my heart and body together in a loving sexual relationship. For the time being, I did sexually what I had always done emotionally: disconnect and detach.

I was a reckless teenager and took dangerous risks, not least of which was driving home from the beach blazing on acid, hanging out the driver's window going 70 mph in the fast lane while steering the wheel with my foot. I managed to escape any serious bad trips, (save an angel dust episode in Newport Beach where I experienced myself melting in a mirror and ran screaming from the bathroom). I also escaped a few close calls with the cops while stoned out of my mind—for instance, the time they pulled us over and ignored the billowing marijuana smoke in exchange for the addresses of the parties we were heading to. We sold our souls and our friends at those parties that night to be set free, and spent the rest of the night getting even more stoned at the local park. I was lucky to have escaped HIV; just a few years later, and my fate most certainly would have been different. Not all of my friends were so lucky. My date at the senior prom, the son of a well-known fashion designer, died of AIDS some years later. I hated Los Angeles and couldn't wait to get out. The summer I graduated high school I moved to San Francisco and never looked back.

CHAPTER 4

Spiritual Awakening

FROM MY FIFTY-YEAR-OLD vantage point, I have come to trust in an elegance, a kind of divine plan, for how things unfold—a wisdom far greater than I could ever consciously plan for myself.

When I moved to San Francisco in the summer of 1979, I entered SF State University with a declared undergraduate major in Broadcast Journalism. I had long harbored a dream to be the next Barbara Walters (years before anyone had heard of Oprah). In fact, in my mid-teens, I had written to both Walters and Phil Donohue letting them know of my ambitions and seeking their guidance. I never heard back from either. Undaunted, I entered college determined to pursue my dreams in broadcasting as a talk-show host. For my freshman assignment, I created a commercial for "Manly," a fictitious birth control product for men. It was a huge success with the class and the professor, but I suffered terrible stage fright on camera.

During my first few years away from L.A., living in college dorms, I felt like a kid in a candy store. The whole world opened up for me. For the first time in my life, my peers were actually interested in something other than sex, drugs, and rock-n-roll. These kids were socially and politically educated, aware, and engaged. I got involved in campus activist groups, such as Students For A Democratic Society, and Marxist groups trying to change the world. While I sympathized with some of their ideologies, I eventually grew frustrated with the hostility, arguing, and in-fighting that seemed to replicate much of what they were trying to fight against. I believed then, as I do now, that *how* you conduct yourself is as important, if not more so, than the message you are trying to convey. In their attempts to change the world, many of these activists were every bit as violent and abusive as the ills they sought to eradicate.

Around this time, I had my second bona fide spontaneous *spiritual awakening*. To help support myself through college, I worked part-time in a well-known flower shop in San Francisco. That Easter Sunday I was terribly bored—all the customers had already bought their Easter flowers and the store was empty. My boss wouldn't let me go home so, in sheer desperation and, guided by some "higher" power, I wandered to the garden in the back of the shop where the flowers were grown. I had never been back there before or after. For some reason, I felt compelled to put my hands in the dirt and start weeding, something I had also never done before because I didn't like getting my hands dirty.

As I dug in the dirt, I was suddenly enveloped in a feeling of immense, universal, radiant, and unconditional love. I remember lifting my eyes to look at a colleague climbing a tree to cut down a vine, and feeling such an overwhelming sense of rapture, awe, wonder, and beauty; it was almost unbearable to behold. I felt all the invisible boundaries separating me from the Divine melt away, and I *knew* I was part of something much greater than what my ordinary senses reveal. The realization remains with me today, as clear as ever: We are all *one,* all individual expressions of one unconditionally loving presence, the Source of everything and everyone, including me. I also undeniably knew that *this* was reality, and the rest of what I had experienced until then was illusion, what the Hindus call *maya.* I knew with certainty that this experience was always present and available. Like a flowing river, I just needed to step into it. Many Gnostic and other spiritual texts describe such transformative moments as spontaneous *numinous* experiences. For this non-practicing Jew, it was as if I had had a direct experience of being bathed in "Christ consciousness" and unconditional love. The fact that it was Easter Sunday, the day of Jesus' resurrection *in the Garden,* didn't escape me.

Still bathed in this numinous glow, I stood up to greet some customers who had entered the store. I remember thinking, "I don't want to lose this experience," and no sooner than I had the thought, the feeling evaporated, the usual veils of illusion returned, and I was once again in my ordinary state of consciousness. Later that night at home, I remembered a similar numinous experience when I was just seven, while lying in the grass of our backyard. I remembered gazing up at the sky, experiencing the veils parting, and having a direct and undeniable experience of a Mystery I was most definitely part of, but that was beyond my capacity to understand. I knew then, too, that I was connected to everything—that we are all connected to something infinite and much more beautiful and loving than the human mind can possibly comprehend.

Years later, remembering this experience helped me to understand why, beginning at the young age of nine, I was compelled to read all of Carlos Castaneda's books on non-ordinary "separate" realities, and why, at that age, they made perfect sense to me. Much later, an eighty-year-old Jungian analyst told me I was probably born Gnostic in this life-time, attuned and forever connected to the Grand Mystery. Whether or not this is so, I do know that my life has always been propelled by a deep hunger, a profound longing and de-sire to know the Mystery as deeply and as intimately as I possibly can, and to live my life in accord with it.

I was born into a home where my Judaic roots had been renounced since my grandmother's generation and, as a re-sult, I had no exposure to religion or spirituality growing up. Because my father had remarried a *shiksa*, we celebrated Christmas in our home with a tree, Christmas carols playing on the stereo, and bagels with cream cheese and lox for break-fast. To this day, I still repeat this Christmas morning ritual.

My childhood home lacked any symbols or images of the divine; I grew up in a spiritual wasteland. Nothing in my home environment helped me make sense of my backyard numinous experience. Absent any affirmation or support, I mentioned it to no one, and that childhood moment went underground until it resurfaced fifteen years later when, on

Easter Sunday in the flower-shop garden, I shoved my hands into the soil, and had my second encounter with the Divine.

Around this time, two seemingly random events occurred that really did alter the course of my life forever. Because of the intense emotional bond I felt with my father, I felt compelled to take an undergraduate elective course called, "Fathers and Daughters in Literature." As an assignment, I had to find a book that addressed the theme of a father-daughter relationship. I was "guided" to a semi-autobiographical novel by French author Anais Nin, whom I had never heard of before. As I recall, Nin's leading character had been abandoned by her father around the same age I was when my mother left; and, surprisingly, he returned home at around the same age I was when my mother returned. There are times in life when it just feels like something greater than you is guiding you and lending you a hand.

How I found my way to this little-known book I don't know. But it felt like the story was meant for me. The character talks about how easily she feels abandoned, unloved, forgotten, discarded, and unworthy. An unreturned phone call from a friend would be interpreted as certain abandonment, as if she had done something wrong, unforgiveable, and was being rejected. Only then, for the first time, it occurred to me that my mother's early abandonment of me might influence and distort the way I perceived myself and how I interpreted and responded to my life and the people in it. Until I read Nin's book, an unreturned phone call couldn't have meant anything *other* than I had done something wrong and was, therefore, unwanted. The possibility that the other person was simply busy and hadn't had a chance to get back to me yet just did not exist in my psyche. Unconsciously, I automatically interpreted events in my life through the lens of my wounded childhood.

Many of us have experienced some degree of childhood trauma and, consequently, we are all part of the "walking wounded"—until we seek counseling or guidance of some kind. We look out at life through childhood lenses that distort how we see ourselves and others, shaping our attitudes to love, trust, and God. We grow up believing we live in a world that is inherently good or evil, safe or unsafe. The danger, of course, is that we believe our interpretations to be real; they go unquestioned or unchallenged, and remain mostly unconscious. It is a delusion of the grandest order that can cause us, and the others around us, a great deal of pain and suffering.

The possibility that an unreturned phone call could mean something other than I had done something wrong and was being abandoned was utterly liberating and awakening—but it also told me I had much work to do to heal my childhood wounds. The legacy of my mother's abandonment not only left me prone to easily feeling abandoned, but also with an eroded sense of self worth.

Imperfect or dysfunctional parenting confronts children with a psychic dilemma far greater than their young, fragile psyches can accommodate. Whenever a parent (or other primary caregiver) abandons or rejects a child, or is emotionally unavailable, violent, or abusive, the young, and utterly dependent psyche of the child cannot comprehend this intolerable failure of adequate parenting. Instead of consciously accepting the fact that the all-important caregiver fails to take care of us, our young minds make an abrupt U-turn and place the blame squarely upon ourselves. Emotionally, we take the "easier" route and tell ourselves, "I must be unworthy, undeserving of love, because I'm inherently flawed, broken, or bad . . ." Such self-blame is "safer" than believing the people we utterly depend on are unsafe or, worse, hurtful and damaging. Rather than experience the world as unsafe or harmful, the child blames herself, unconsciously preserving the illusion of a safe world. The fragile young psyche needs to believe this, even in the face of abuse. However, in cases of extreme abuse, violence, or neglect, the child's psyche can shatter.

While this strategy of adopting the blame to preserve a sense of safety in a big and terrifying world helps us to survive, it also begins an insidious and corrosive attack on the child's developing sense of self and self-worth. Without knowing it, we begin to believe we are flawed and unworthy; that we are to blame for what others have done to us; that we deserved it because we are inherently bad, unlovable, and undeserving. Without conscious awareness of these faulty beliefs about ourselves lurking in the recesses of our psyches, we can contaminate all our future relationships with a dysfunctional mix of deficiency, self-doubt, insecurity, and feelings of worthlessness.

Around this time, a second serendipitous event also happened: I enrolled in an undergraduate English Composition course taught by a Zen Buddhist psychologist. He was to become the first of many in a great line of mentors who changed, shaped, and inspired me forever. In addition to teaching English composition courses, he also ran a peer counseling program, the Center For Institutional Change (CIC), on campus that allowed students studying psychology to be staff members and to learn, experientially, how to counsel others. It was an innovative program, and I became a staff member for four years. During this period, I also got myself into therapy for the first time, and, as a result, changed my major from Broadcast Journalism to Psychology. I was awakening, turned on by self-discovery, and plowed headlong into my future profession.

Each morning, the CIC staff sat in a circle on the floor on pillows, meditated together, and then "checked-in." This regular morning practice helped us to connect with ourselves deeply, and to find language to authentically and vulnerably express our feelings and thoughts in the moment. Today, many years later, I continue to find it natural to keep up this practice—it helps me to know more clearly what I am feeling, and gives me the words I need to express who I am. Having had a childhood where I learned *not to know* what I was feeling—and certainly not to express it—this element of my awakening was revolutionary.

Terrifying at first, and then confusing, in time it became exhilarating. To be able to "find" myself emotionally—to connect with my feelings, and develop the courage to express myself to a group of peers—healed wounds I didn't even know I had. During my tenure at CIC, our group laughed, cried, fought, and loved each other; we also taught each other how to be in honest, open, vulnerable, trusting, and mature relationships.

While working at CIC, I entered therapy for the first time, with a very sweet and loving woman named Donna. Starting in my twenties, my first years of therapy focused on my experience of being abandoned by my mother and the long shadow of its emotional aftermath. Not until my late thirties would I seriously take on the even more challenging and insidious legacy of my relationship with my father.

My time with Donna began by slowly unpacking the emotional wreckage of my mother's abandonment. I told and retold my story, describing how my mother had walked out the door when I was just under two-and-a-half. Initially, despite the major trauma of this event, I remained utterly devoid of feelings as I shared my story—as if summarizing a movie I had seen, not a true and painful story *I had lived*.

Eventually, after about a year, the feelings finally arrived. I went into my session as usual, talking about, and bemoaning, what I was looking for in a relationship with a man. Donna looked at me:

"You must really have not gotten what you needed as a child to be wanting and needing that so desperately."

I immediately reacted with a strong physical sensation: I felt her words enter my ears, rattle about in my head, travel down my neck, and then hit a solid block of frozen ice below. Everything in me felt cold, hard, and unyielding—blocking out all emotions.

After the session, I went home to the apartment I shared with my best friend in San Francisco's Haight Ashbury district. She was away for the weekend with her boyfriend and I was all alone. I sat on the edge of my bed and could feel what seemed like a volcano about to erupt from the depths of my psyche. I had no idea what was about to happen, but I remember looking around my room and assessing that, whatever was about to explode, I would be safe here. I crawled into bed, pulled the covers up over my head, and waited . . . and waited . . . and waited.

At some point, the block of ice in my heart and gut began to thaw. Without knowing why, I began sobbing . . . and sobbing . . . and sobbing. Had the walls not been sound-proofed, my guttural, primitive, moaning and wailing would have startled the neighbors. I'm sure it sounded like I was being tortured. A tsunami of twenty-plus years of repressed feelings and memories broke through into my consciousness. Painful memories of the day my mother left, waking up without her, not knowing what had happened or why, flooded my awareness. I remembered exactly what I looked like, the apartment, what my dad was doing. The recollection was so strong I felt I was "re-experiencing" those images and emotions *consciously for the first time*—the shattering of my world, the unbearable sense of loss, grief, hurt, loneliness, confusion, and despair. I cried until I fell asleep.

Next morning, at the CIC staff check-in, I tearfully shared what had happened. Recognizing I was in a process of thawing previously frozen and repressed childhood memories and feelings, my colleagues agreed to take my counseling clients for the next few weeks, and encouraged me to use the pillow-cushioned room as a safe space to cry and let the grieving move through me. I believed I would cry in there forever. The pain, anguish, and grief were more than I could bear—at least, that's what it felt like. Years later, another dear mentor of mine confided that although she had tried to cry forever, it was humanly impossible. I found those words deeply comforting.

After a couple weeks of sobbing in the comfort and safety of that pillow-filled womb, I emerged anew—tender, shaken, and vulnerable, but profoundly connected to the truth of my story and my feelings about it. At this point, my birth mother was living in Massachusetts where I would periodically visit her in a continuation of the fairy tale, make-believe relationship we had been having since her return when I was eleven. Following my emotional "Big Thaw," I decided to visit her. By now, I had many questions to ask, and many feelings to express. She had no idea what was coming.

When she met me at the gate at Boston's Logan airport, I semiconsciously sized her up, and decided she looked emotionally strong enough to withstand the pending onslaught—an explosion of twenty-plus years of suppressed feelings and questions, feelings she had never had to deal with. Good girls don't say such things.

Even before we stepped inside her front door, the torrent erupted. As we got out of the car with my luggage, we heard a woman across the street yelling at her child. My mother made some comment about what a terrible mother that woman was—just the spark I needed to detonate the TNT in my wounded psyche. As we entered through the screen door, I screamed: "WHO THE FUCK DO YOU THINK YOU ARE COMMENTING ON THAT WOMAN'S MOTHERING? WHAT THE FUCK KIND OF MOTHER WERE YOU? YOU WALKED OUT ON ME WHEN I WAS TWO-AND-HALF YEARS OLD, AND I DIDN'T SEE YOU AGAIN UNTIL I WAS ELEVEN. WHERE THE FUCK WERE YOU ALL OF THOSE YEARS? HOW COULD YOU DO THAT TO ME? FUCK YOU! I HATE YOU!!! And that was just the prelude . . .

A two-day marathon ensued, without breaks for sleep, water, or food. We talked about all of the things we'd never said to each other before. She sat me down on her bed, said to me, "I knew this day would eventually come"—and, to her credit, took the full force of my long-pent up fury and rage. She listened. She allowed me to spew out all the hurt, anger, rage, and confusion. She answered every one of my endless questions; she explained to me who she had been back then, why she felt she had to leave, why she stayed away, and why she came back.

She told me the story of her own painful, abusive, and traumatic childhood: about her mother's affair with her later-to-be stepfather; about how her mother had planned to leave the two girls with their father, and about the blunt abandonment note, "The kids are yours; I don't want them"—on the very day her father was inconveniently killed in the famous Cocoanut Grove fire. She told me about how she and her sister were reluctantly retrieved by her mother and her lover who had just tried to unload them, and how, from then on, they were treated with unspeakable resentment, physical, emotional, and sexual abuse; how she and her sister were locked in closets for days without food or water, left to excrete on themselves, tormented and taunted from the other side of the door while they clung desperately to each other; how, when the door would finally open, her mother's lover would sexually abuse them while her mother laughed and watched.

She told me how, when I was about two-years-old, she feared she would abuse me just as her mother had done to her. This fear—amplified by a debilitating dread that I would grow up to hate her as much as she had grown to hate her own mother and now herself—paralyzed her. She knew she couldn't be the kind of mother I needed and deserved, and she trusted my father to find a woman who could. She left us in the middle of the night, spent the first few months with friends, so emotionally distraught she almost killed herself, and then eventually found her way to Hawaii and Puerto Rico where she had lived and worked as a jazz singer.

She told me she sobbed every year on my birthday, and how every time she saw a girl roughly my age, her heart would break, and she would wonder how I was doing, if my dad had remarried, and if I was happy and healthy. She told me she had come back into my life after her mom died because she didn't want me to grow up without having a chance to heal the damage she had caused. She didn't know if I would want contact with her, or if my father would allow it, but at least she wanted to bring herself to the healing table to make it possible—and she had waited all these years for me to be ready. We laughed, we cried, and we held each other until we were exhausted from the ordeal.

I will remain forever grateful to her for her ability and willingness to bear witness to my pain and anger; for allowing me to confront her—despite her own feelings of pain, loss, guilt, and shame for the choices she had made, and the pain it had caused us both; and for taking responsibility for the damage she had caused. Rarely, when children of trauma find the courage to confront their parents or perpetrators, do they receive such a gracious response. More often than not, they are re-traumatized by denials, blame, and more emotional abuse or neglect. A crucial part of my healing resulted from the extreme good fortune that, when it mattered most, my mother had the emotional fortitude and presence, grace and generosity, to validate and honor the pain I finally expressed. Today, I owe her profound gratitude not only for having given me life itself, but also for being able and willing to have validated, honored, and shared my pain when I was finally able and willing to bring it to her.

CHAPTER 5

Love, Sex, and Human Potential

AFTER GRADUATING *SUMMA* cum laude with a bachelor's degree in psychology, I decided to go live with my birth mother and her best friend in Massachusetts while going to graduate school. I wanted—as she did—to find out what kind of relationship we actually had now that we were honest, authentic, and open with each other. Although I got accepted to Harvard's Master Degree program in psychology, I opted for a smaller, lesser-known university in Cambridge. Lesley College Graduate School's experientially based program allowed me to work with *human beings* rather than rats in a lab. Understandably, my family was proud that Harvard had accepted me, and so they made a pin for me to wear: "I Turned Down Harvard." This was one of the many times in life I followed my own path—the road less traveled, rather than the more socially prestigious one.

The Lesley College Graduate program was an ideal fit for me, not least because I had many great teachers and mentors there. The opportunity to work with different client populations—including children, families, adolescents, and people with extreme mental disorders—allowed me to discover my natural talents at listening to, understanding, and providing empathy and healing to others. My relationship with my mom, however, proved less than ideal. I discovered how severely emotionally damaged she was because of her abusive childhood. She was prone to paranoia and suspicion; for example, often imagining that her friend and I secretly talked about her behind her back while watching TV. She would fly off into angry outbursts and hostile rants, and, no matter what we said, we found it impossible to assuage her paranoia. After a year living together, she accepted a job as an editor with *Surfer Magazine* in Southern California, and she and her friend moved. I couldn't have been more relieved.

Not long after, while attending Lesley, and working at Harvard in the Development/Alumni Relations Department, a school colleague introduced me to the man who would become my husband. Betsy and I were sitting around with some women friends bemoaning the sorry state of our relationships, wondering why we couldn't find a decent man. A couple of days later, I got a phone call from a guy who said Betsy had given him my number because we might like to get to know each other—would I like to come to a Trivial Pursuits party (all the rage at the time)?

Deep into my studies and finals, preparing for a vacation with my family in Hawaii in a few weeks, and studying scuba diving for the upcoming trip, I had a full plate and politely declined. Something told me I would hear from him again, and sure enough, a few days after the party, he called again. This time, we talked for hours, covering a wide range of topics—from politics and religion, to beliefs, attitudes, feelings, about all kinds of "things that matter." Keith was the first man I felt I could really talk with intimately and deeply; we both seemed to think and feel in similar ways. During that long conversation, something he said opened my heart to the possibility of a relationship between us.

At one point, I said, "You know, it's just not satisfying looking into a phone receiver any longer. Why don't we make a date to actually meet each other in person?"

Later, he told me that my boldness and candor were a huge turn-on for him, opening his heart to whatever possibilities might lie ahead. We scheduled a date for a few nights later. In the meantime, because I *happened* to work in the Harvard Alumni office, and he *happened* to have gotten his doctorate from Harvard, I was able to look up his records and check the guy out. A girl's gotta do what a girl's gotta do! Nowadays, with Google and Facebook, we have everything at our fingertips in seconds. I was duly impressed with what I saw.

We met in Cambridge Square for Chinese dinner, and strolled around afterwards. By midnight, sitting on a bench engrossed in intimate conversation, we began to envision our future together. A few days later, I left for my family vacation in Hawaii and he left for his family vacation on the Jersey shore. Lying on the beach in Maui, I confided to my sister: "I've just met the man I'm going to marry." At the same time, as he told me later, he was lying on the Jersey beach with his siblings, telling them: "I've just met the woman I'm going to marry." We returned from our mutual vacations to our second date.

Things moved so fast, I said to him: "If we don't slow this train down, I'm going to bolt. We've only had one date, and already our fantasies are flying far off into the future. We've got to slow down and build a foundation upon which these fantasies can stand."

He honored my need to slow down, and I trusted him even more. Nevertheless, within six months we had moved in together (there's slow . . . and then there's *sloooowwwww*).

Finally, I was with a man I could tell anything to, knowing he would listen empathically. I remember the night I tested him with my "big reveal." While we were dating, I worked at a difficult job dealing with extremely disturbed mentally ill patients. Each day arriving at work, I never knew what to expect—perhaps I would find someone had hanged himself, or had tried to, or someone had burned herself on the arms with cigarette butts, or someone would fly into a paranoid psychotic rage. . . . In an effort to come down at the end of the work week, I would often sequester myself in my bedroom and "go crazy"—eating really bad, disgusting food and staying in bed all night watching TV. I felt ashamed to share this "worst secret." What if he thought I really was crazy, and then abandoned me? I set the stage for the big reveal by forewarning him I had a horrible secret that he must know about me if he was really going to go any further in this relationship. He must have thought I was about to confess to being a murderer. When I finally outed myself, he lovingly smiled, took me in his arms, and told me he could understand why I would need a way to "come down" at the end of the week. Given my nerve-wracking job, he viewed such self-indulgence as normal and restorative—despite the disgusting food—a healthy way to decompress from a stressful week. What a relief to discover he loved me anyway, even knowing my "big secret."

Within two years, after I completed my master's degree, we got married. As a girl, I never longed to grow up and get married. I never clipped out magazine pictures of brides, waiting for my own big wedding day. Instead, I had aspired to have a career. The *idea* of marriage never appealed to me. However, once I fell in love and wanted to share my life with this man, *then* marriage made sense to me.

We married at a beautiful inn on the ocean in Cape Ann, Massachusetts. Both my moms were there, and my father and stepmother walked me down the aisle. My birth mother sang, "Is This The Little Girl I Carried" from *Fiddler On The Roof* at the reception. This felt like the best, most authentic, way to honor the role both women had played in my life.

Our marriage wasn't perfect, even from the beginning—but what relationship is? We have always been close friends, and he has always been my greatest advocate, believing in and supporting my dreams. However, as it turned out, he had his own childhood traumas with lingering aftereffects. He had grown up in what he described as an emotionally cold family: a mother who gave no physical affection, and a narcissistic and emotionally overbearing father. His parents divorced when he was young, remarried and divorced again, and are now both on their third marriages. His family tree is so complex, it took me months to comprehend it. Keith had survived the emotional wasteland of his childhood by detaching and disconnecting, just as my father had done. I had fallen in love with his capacity to be emotionally "present" with me while we were dating, but within the container of a committed marriage our respective childhood wounds erupted, and our strategies for coping with them returned.

From the beginning, we struggled with sexual incompatibility. I was then, and still am, a highly sexual being. For the first time in my life, I was deeply in love with my sexual partner, and I wanted to make love frequently—a joyful and deep way to connect with the man I loved. My exuberant desire for lovemaking challenged him, and he began to subtly shame me rather than take responsibility for being challenged by the intimacy. As a result, I silently began to sexually withdraw and shut down, from myself as much as from him.

As early as our honeymoon in Greece, our marriage commitment began to frighten him, and he withdrew emotionally, leaving me, once again, feeling abandoned and bewildered. With sufficient maturity and understanding of what was happening between us and why, I'm certain we would have dealt with things much differently. Re-traumatized by feeling abandoned yet again, I emotionally withdrew from the marriage to protect myself. Rather than knowing how to vulnerably express my feelings of abandonment, I either withdrew or lashed out in anger and resentment. More often than not, during the course of our marriage, my anger surfaced more than my hurt—and, naturally, this caused him to emotionally withdraw even further.

As happens for many couples, our marriage became a perfect storm. I've worked with couples for more than twenty-five years and am constantly surprised, if not amazed, at how the unconscious mind works. In intimate relationships, straight or gay, we often unconsciously try to heal childhood wounds. Whatever we consciously look for in a partner, the unconscious works in devious ways, driving us to pick a partner who will, unwittingly, wound us in exactly the ways we were traumatized as a child. While committed relationships can be—and usually are—challenging, nevertheless the greater the test the greater the *opportunity* to find a more mature and healthy way to respond, beyond how we did as a child. At least, that's the theory. Unfortunately, more often than not, both partners re-traumatize each other, using the same childhood defenses, leading the couple into a vicious cycle of hurting each other. By bringing dysfunctional childhood patterns to consciousness we can begin to make different choices.

In our case, we believed our relationship to be our spiritual path, and that's how we approached it. We rolled up our sleeves, dived into the fray, and tried as best we could to understand ourselves and each other. We went to couples counseling together, struggled to understand our triggers, and learned more effective ways to communicate with each other, vulnerably and with accountability.

After graduating with my master's degree, I got accepted into a doctoral program in psychology at the California

School of Professional Psychology in Alameda, California, so we moved back to the Bay Area and set up house as husband and wife. Not long into my doctoral program, I enrolled in a three-and-a-half-day consciousness seminar recommended by my husband's employer. As I sat in the hotel room, watching the workshop conductor lead the seminar, I knew I had found my life's calling: I wanted to be a workshop conductor. In a room of about 150, many people, including me, experienced profound emotional breakthroughs, and a great deal of healing occurred throughout the weekend. From the first evening, I knew some form of life coaching or transformational counseling would be my life's calling—and I knew I could do it. I also knew that my particularly Freudian doctoral program in psychology would not prepare me for this kind of deep experiential, life-transforming work. The seminar ended on Sunday night. By Monday morning, I had quit the doctoral program, and by Wednesday night I had declared to the seminar company staff that I wanted to be a workshop conductor. A few months later, I was hired, and never looked back. Once again, I had followed my own inner promptings, bucked convention, and had chosen the "road less traveled."

Founded by a charismatic and brilliant man, with a mission to transform and empower people's lives, the workshop company nevertheless struggled with an internal culture of emotional abuse—from senior management to staff. I have since discovered that abuse of power runs rampant with charismatic, narcissistic leaders. One day, I witnessed a senior executive publically berate an employee and then spit on him.

From then on, I wanted nothing to do with a company that taught how to have healthy, emotionally responsible relationships, but didn't practice what it preached—so I left.

I had intended to create my own consciousness seminar company when I discovered another woman who had also left the same company, for the same reasons. Disillusioned, she had started her own seminar company. We decided to join forces. Unknown to me at the time, I was newly pregnant with my first child. We joyfully continued to teach seminars together throughout my pregnancy, and into the first months of my son's life. However, the almost three-hour commute each way became too great a hardship with an infant. Besides, although I had had every intention of being a working mom, once my son was born, I wanted only to sit with him in my arms and stare into his beautiful face.

My son's birth was a revolution of love—*Le Grand Love Affaire*. Never before had I felt such a rapturous explosion of unconditional love. I spent hours holding him in my arms, nursing him, singing and cooing to him, surrounded in a bubble of pure love and delight. During my pregnancy, I felt physically better than at any other time in my life. This all changed, of course, when hard labor kicked in and I experienced my first whopping contraction. I turned to my husband and said, with all sincerity, "I've changed my mind. Take me home. I don't want to do this!" Other than that moment of temporary insanity, my pregnancy, labor, and delivery were a breeze. During my pregnancy, I craved egg salad sandwiches—that's all I wanted. My son's personality is very much like an egg salad: calm and chill. His eleventh-grade psychology teacher told me many years later, after giving the kids a chance to experiment with a biofeedback machine, that she had never met anyone before my son whose natural resting state was like a seasoned Zen meditator—egg salad!

In stark contrast, ten years later, pregnant with my daughter, I craved only spicy foods. And, unlike her chill brother, she is a spicy one!

After nine months of staring into my beautiful baby boy's eyes, I began to feel the need for some outside adult stimulation, so decided to return to work part-time. Thinking I'd give business consulting a try, I got hired working as a workshop conductor for an employee assistance program, designing and delivering workshops. I taught stress management, time management, and understanding and working with different personality styles to a variety of San Francisco law firms. But the day I taught a workshop on how to conduct performance evaluations to middle managers at Jiffy Lube I sadly had to admit to myself that my life's purpose lay in a different direction. Leading corporate workshops tended to frustrate me because, unlike facilitating transformational seminars, some topics and responses were clearly "off limits." With my background in psychology plus experience leading seminars, I could see more deeply into people's personalities and emotional blockages—but in a business setting I didn't have permission to address their issues head-on, and this limited my effectiveness to help facilitate any major or lasting change. Honoring what I love to do, I decided to return to personal growth workshops and seminars, where I could go really deep with participants.

With due diligence, I researched companies offering consciousness workshops. I found many, and traveled around the country observing and, in some cases, participating in seminars. As fate or luck would have it, the company that best fit my needs and preferences turned out to be in my own backyard. Founded and run by two women, it integrated consciousness development techniques from other companies with depth psychology—an approach I highly valued. I immediately felt at home.

This company viewed itself as a modern-day "mystery school," teaching not only psychological skills for healing and well-being, but also ways to enter the "mystery of life" and to cultivate a relationship with the Divine. I flourished during my tenure there, and delighted in the wide variety of topics I could teach using different formats and techniques—including retreats for women, couples, meditation, chakra initiation, relationship skill building, goal setting and achievement, plus a lot more. I reveled in the opportunity to blend my psychological and spiritual passions.

Unfortunately, once again, one of the women founders proved to be yet another brilliant, charismatic, but emotionally abusive and narcissistic leader. However, because I loved the work so much, and had cultivated valuable relationships with my students, I continued on for several years before leaving. During this time, I also entered therapy again, and began to unravel the legacy of my relationship with my father.

My father, at times warm, loving, and affectionate, could also be emotionally demeaning, belittling, and misogynistic. He made fun of me as far back as I can remember, cracking condescending jokes about my first crush on a boy, teasing me painfully when I began menstruation, making demeaning comments about my body, and telling me often that I was, "a little shit; what do you know." He often disguised his put-downs as humor, and it took years in therapy before I could see that even when something is said in humor, it can still hurt and be emotionally corrosive to a little girl. He frequently made demeaning and sexualized comments to me about other women, "Oh, look at her ass; what a quiff." He regaled everyone in the family with repeated stories of his sexual conquests when he was younger, some of which detailed his willingness to "shtoop raw bizone," a phrase he had invented to describe a particularly ugly conquest.

As I had learned to do when my mother left, I suppressed how his comments made me feel. I laughed at his jokes, I encouraged his humor, I fed his narcissism, and I listened attentively to his repeated stories of sexual conquests and belittling comments about women, including me. I needed desperately to believe in my father as my hero—so much, in fact, I denied anything that contradicted my "hero illusion," opting instead to fiercely defend him. Until well into my thirties, I could not risk cracking the walls of denial; only then did I begin to see him more clearly.

Around this time, I entered therapy with a very dear, older, Jungian analyst, who helped me to not only see my father with clear eyes, but to repair the debilitating damage he had done to my sense of self worth. Because my father valued only what was scientific, rational, provable, and verifiable, he expressed contempt for anything psychological, emotional, or spiritual. Essentially, he disdained anything *feminine*— including intuitive, non-linear ways of knowing and being. Emotionally and spiritually, I became the object of his projections—everything feminine or spiritual he denied or feared about himself—his "Shadow"—he projected as a flaw or failing onto *me*.

Perhaps because of these long-standing and traumatic experiences, I developed an early interest in matters of the soul, and eventually created a successful career in psychology, dealing with emotions and spirituality. True to form, my father missed no opportunity to slander my work or my clients. He would often say such things as, "How many wimps did you see today? Why do they pay you to talk to them; what do you know; What could you possibly have to offer them?" At the time, I didn't know how badly he had eroded my self-worth, but I did feel a great deal of pain and self-doubt about who I was and the value of what I had to offer.

How does a girl, whose father had nothing but contempt for the feminine, value herself? My greatest strengths and gifts are my ability to empathically understand another person's emotional reality, my ability to intuitively read the emotional climate of a workshop room and respond in ways that are helpful and healing for the participants, along with my ability to be transparent enough to the Mystery that I can feel deeply connected with the Divine. *Not one* of these attributes was recognized or valued by my father. And although those attributes have always been my greatest strengths, deep down I believed they were valueless. The pain of being invisible to him—rejected to my core—debilitated me.

My wonderful eighty-year old Jungian analyst Seymour helped me to see and own who and what I am, and to believe in my inherent value. When I talked glowingly of my father in heroic terms, he pushed back, helping me to crack open that delusional fantasy. He demanded that I see the "soul torture," as he called it, of my father's attitude toward me. Seymour valued my gifts and held them in such high esteem that, eventually, I, too, came to recognize them as important and valuable. Although it took time, I finally understood that my father's contempt for all things feminine stemmed from the frightening emotional instability of his mother. Throughout his childhood, he had been conditioned to view emotions as dangerous and unpredictable, and, out of necessity, he had developed a strong aversion to anything emotional. He also grew up with an ambivalent and conflicted relationship to women—needing and wanting them, and feeling terrified and emotionally overwhelmed by them, all at the same time.

Quieting my father's voice of contempt inside my own head turned out to be a long, arduous, and painful journey. Filled with self-loathing, one by one, I had to confront and contend with each of the howling demons. For a long time, I felt they would win the battle for my soul. The emotional-spiritual bloodbath reminded me of the Hindu epic

Mahabharata, depicting warfare between good and evil. Battered, bloodied, and weary, I finally glimpsed a ray of hope. This lifeline, recorded as a journal entry from meditation imagery I had during my time in Jungian therapy, best illustrates what happened:

I speak to you now as Warrior Woman. My name is Tummo. Only now can I speak of the journey I have taken. I have walked barefooted and open-eyed through the desert fire. I have been burned to ash and resurrected anew. I have been attacked and beaten by the fiercest of demons, shadows, tricksters, and cons, and have stared each and every one of them squarely in their evil-filled eyes, and have lived to tell the tale. Here is my story:

It begins when my husband and I sought the guidance and counsel of a wise elder. In our first meetings with him, my heart cried aloud at the emptiness in our marriage. My heart ached to feel connected to my husband as the great gods and goddesses are joined together. I writhed in the agony of my aloneness and ranted at the elder to earn my respect by giving me answers and showing me the way. He laughed at my silly demands and steadfastly offered me nothing more than patience and an unwavering trust in my own ability to find my way home.

Early on, the gods visited me in a dream. A Bacchus-like half-man-half-beast tried to kill me.

As the dream shifted, we turned into actors on a Shakespearean stage portraying lovers. Still terrified of the beast, I nevertheless enacted our love scene, and by the time we left the stage, we were joined together truly as lovers. When I awoke from this dream, I knew that it reflected my journey with the elder and his wise counsel: I must confront the demon who has been trying to kill me and who will become my sacred lover.

I spent many months, even years, yearning for this sacred lover and agonizing in despair at my husband's failure to fulfill that yearning. In utter despair and resignation, I turned my eyes toward the elder and yearned for him to be my divine partner. My desire for him burns my eyes, shatters my heart, breaks my bones, and leaves me so bereft that I know I will surely die. I want to. I cannot live with this desire burning a hole in my being. It can't be withstood. I am sure of it. The elder tells me to wait, to trust. I am dying a slow and torturous death and I have nothing left to hold onto. I am starved and thirsty and have nothing to nourish me. The elder tells me again and again to wait, to trust. I try feebly over and over and over again to turn my eyes toward my husband, toward the elder, toward somebody—*anybody*—who will feed this hunger in me and satiate the desire. I rail, demand, and hope until all hope is gone. No one will come to rescue me. No one will feed this hunger. In this despair, I know for certain I will die. This cannot be endured. And yet each day I awake with my life before me to be lived. I am stumbling and choking on the dry desert air. No life exists here.

And then the gods visit me once again in a dream. I am traveling in India and an enormous, one-hundred-foot-long snake writhes its way across my path. I awake knowing some big force is breaking through in me. I cannot avoid it; it is directly in front of my path.

In my last desperate attempt to live, to breathe, to survive, I begin to focus my eyes inward. To contemplate the possibility that that is the only place left I have not yet looked for sustenance. I have nothing else left to lose. In desperation, I turn my gaze inward, which seems to delight the elder greatly. He celebrates each minute, painstaking, yet nourishing, inner self-glimpse I get. He demands that I honor and acknowledge all the gods and demons that live within me. He is relentless. He will not let me ignore either the gods or the demons. He insists that I pay rightful homage to the great gods, but the demons won't let me—these demons my own father planted inside my soul.

The Great War begins. Once again, I am left battered and bloodied on the battlefield. The demons are winning, feasting on the taste of my blood. The gods are crying. Who will lead this battle on? Will everything end here? Day and night, the demons howling inside my head torture me. They howl so loud I can barely hear the crying of the gods. Nothing but the ceaseless howling remains. I cannot match these demons, and so, once again, death comes for me. I have no strength to fight any more.

Just when I am certain the next blow will kill me the miracle happens. In an instant that took an eternity, I see the demons for what they are, and from within the core of my being the Warrior Woman rises up, fierce and tall and strong and proud. Larger than any demon on the battlefield, her presence reduces them to pitiless mangy dogs cowering and scurrying away. I am she. I am that fierce and proud Warrioress. The gods and I bow to each other. My name is Tummo.

It took another fifteen years for me to serendipitously discover that in Tibetan, the word *Tummo* literally means, "Fierce Woman!" How my psyche knew that, I have absolutely no idea!

In therapeutic work, sometimes the conscious mind cannot resolve a particular dilemma—especially when the ego (our precious self-identity), needs to take a back seat, but refuses to give up without a fight. And such internal battles can get quite nasty for the client, who fears she will die—or wants to. The intense pain can feel unbearable. Defense mechanisms, entrenched since early childhood, spring into action, desperately trying to keep the psyche from shattering. Based on my own journey, and from watching hundreds of clients over the years, I know that if one can bear this tension, and withstand the many "dark nights of the soul," a new self will begin to emerge, more psychologically and spiritually whole and intact. Just like an actual birth, this kind of psycho-spiritual "rebirth" can be treacherous as the client squeezes through an existential "birth-canal" into a new way of being. Like a baby being born, the psyche resists relinquishing all that has kept it safe until now—a trade-off for some future unknown possibility. As the psychic metamorphosis unfolds, sometimes all the client can do is hang on for dear life and ride it out, trusting the outcome will be worth the pain. But tell that to the caterpillar as it enters the chrysalis phase! It must die to itself, sacrificing the old in order for a new self to appear. So it is with psychological and spiritual healing and transformation.

By unconsciously adopting my father's view about my lack of worth, I could psychologically preserve him as my hero. In doing so, I avoided the horror of recognizing that the life raft I had desperately clung to when my mother abandoned me, sometimes became a vicious shark. Alternatively loving and hurtful, the "raft/shark" contradiction confused me. How could the man who loved me, played with me, comforted me in his lap when I fell asleep as a child, kept me safe, be the same man who had systematically eroded my sense of myself and my self-worth? It seemed impossible, yet my father lived it daily.

As Tummo began to take hold in my psyche, my relationship with my father began to change. No longer willing to be the good little daddy's girl who ignored his snide comments, or endured his blatant disregard for my wishes, I began to push back against him. Indeed, I *knew* without a doubt that *The Times They Are A Changing* when he and my sister came to visit me. I had just finished reading Shirley MacLean's *The Camino: A Journey Of The Spirit,* about a spiritual pilgrimage she undertook in Spain, and was telling my sister about it. My father launched into his usual onslaught of contemptuous remarks about all things spiritual, attacking not only Ms. MacLean, but my sister and I as well for believing in such things.

At first, I noticed my habitual tendency to let it slide, but then I realized this man expressed contempt for something he truly did not understand. I had spent the better part of 20 years investigating spiritual matters, and had not only immersed myself in the world's spiritual texts but, by then, also had numerous direct spiritual experiences. Rather than staying silent and accepting I was a "flake," I looked at him with compassion and thought: "How sad that this man may never know the comfort a spiritual reality could give him. How limited his world must be; beyond what he can see with his own eyes or touch with his own hands nothing real exists. How much rapture, awe, and grace will he miss in his lifetime?"

When my stepmother died a few years later, and my father was wracked with blinding grief and desperate to find some relief, he agreed to come with me to see my analyst. I sat in the room watching my dad denounce all things spiritual to this very spiritual man. One particularly poignant exchange had my dad fiercely arguing that God does not exist:

"There is no such thing as God," he protested. "I only believe in what I can see with my own eyes, touch with my own hands."

Seymour responded gently: "Did you love your wife?"

"Well, of course I did."

"How do you see love?" Seymour probed a little deeper. My dad fell silent.

"Have you ever been transfixed by the fragrance of a beautiful rose or been caught in a state of awe witnessing something in nature?" Seymour went on.

"Yes," my father replied with an unusual softness.

"How do you explain the love you felt for your wife or the awe you feel in nature? Can you see love? Can you see awe or rapture? Can you touch it with your hands?"

My father's characteristically contemptuous and quick retorts vanished, and his eyes filled with tears.

"I suppose . . . perhaps you have a point I should consider," he conceded.

I watched my analyst gracefully hold his own truth in the face of my father's contempt and disbelief, and I felt grateful to have a map for how it might look. No more would I devalue myself, my beliefs, my talents, and my gifts in the face of my father's contempt. I had, in psychological jargon, finally begun to emotionally *individuate* from my father.

Part 3

Longing

CHAPTER 6

Soul Time

As MY INNER spiritual journey deepened, I had a greater need for solitude and silence. And as any working mother with children knows, solitude and silence are two rare commodities, indeed! Walking to the beach one day with a group of girlfriends, I complained about how desperately I needed time away for myself . . . not just a one-time getaway, but a regular way of having quiet contemplative time in my everyday life. I didn't see how it could be possible given my busy, crazy schedule, but my soul gasped for solitude like a nomad seeking water in the desert. At various times in life's journey, the soul demands attention. First, it begins as faint whispers that, if denied or ignored, become louder and more urgent. My soul begged for attention.

With the mysterious grace of serendipity, one of my friends turned toward me dangling her house key: "Our house up in the country is vacant every week from Tuesday morning through Wednesday night when we are in the city. Take this key and go up there every week for twenty-four hours of solitude." My jaw dropped—not only because of her generosity, but also because I was struck by the miracle that I could so desperately want something, and then have it handed to me right then and there.

I didn't know if Keith would support this new adventure, as it would place an additional weekly burden on him; but, as always, he was willing to support me in every way. We figured out how to get the kids covered, and I began a two-year odyssey—while still married, working, and with two young children at home—to dive into my own solitude and silence. That period remains both precious and spiritually fruitful for me.

Every Tuesday night, I would go to my ecstatic dance class and then, in blissful silence, drive the hour to my friends' magnificent country home. As soon as I arrived, I would light candles and create a sacred space around me. Then, I'd watch the sunset, meditate, journal, walk, and go to sleep knowing I could sleep until my body naturally woke itself up . . . no alarm clock bugging me to get up with the kids, get their breakfast, and get them to school. I had a relaxing twenty-four hours to settle into my own rhythms and reveries.

As the weeks wore on, my writings deepened, and, with great surprise, I found I could access wisdom waiting within my soul. Leaving behind the hectic pace of my life—teaching, traveling, and raising kids, and unplugging from my phone, computer, and television—even that short weekly "oasis" allowed me to drop into longed-for profound states of meditation and contemplation. I blocked out this period in my calendar as precious "Me Time," and it became inviolable. I preserved and protected this respite like a mother guarding her young. Nothing—not doctor's appointments, teacher conferences, bills, shopping, workshops, or anything else—took priority over "Me Time." To my surprise, everyone—my children, husband, friends, and work colleagues—"recalibrated" around my new schedule just fine. I have since recommended this practice of "Me Time" to many of my clients. Initially, I hear the expected arguments and push-back that they "don't have the time," or "can't possibly make it happen with work, kids, etc.," but inevitably, those who do make the time experience it as a treasure in their lives, something they are willing to fight to preserve.

For the rest of the week, even before I got to the country house, I noticed my mood had changed—a very welcome unexpected benefit. Just knowing I had twenty-four hours of solitude and silence to look forward to, elevated my mood and helped this working mom become less cranky with her kids. I also became more patient with traffic, and in general more relaxed with the often-tedious minutiae of daily life—as if my soul knew "we" had a weekly date, and could relax. The prospect (and later the reality) of significant quiet time made me happier and more joyous, not just during my retreat, but during the rest of my week as well.

As my meditations and contemplations deepened, I noticed a shift in my writing. I began to experience what felt like direct transmissions from "Source." Wisdom, uncluttered and unfiltered by my ego, began pouring out of me and onto the page. I imagine that all Gnostics or mystics throughout time have written from these deep meditative states. Only from there can we access the *akashic* records. According to *Wikipedia*, "The akashic records (*akasha* is a Sanskrit word meaning "sky," "space," or "aether") is a term used in Theosophy (and Anthroposophy) to describe a compendium of mystical knowledge encoded in a non-physical plane of existence."

During a particularly deep meditation, as I engaged in a "writing dialogue" with my soul, I asked: "Tell me, who are you? I want to know you." I include the full dialogue below:

I am deep within your soul. I am your wisdom, your beauty. I have so much I want to say. So much that needs to be said. So much that needs to be heard.

"What do you want to say so badly?" I asked, and my soul responded:

I want to speak only of things that matter. I want to penetrate the veils, to touch people in the deepest places where they can find themselves again, or perhaps fully and deeply for the very first time.

I want people to know themselves as God, to remember who they are.

I want you to remember that I am that God within you; that I can guide you through your life from a place of deep wisdom and knowing.

I want the world to know that this is all so incredibly precious; that each moment is a unique universe with everything in it; that life is to be savored; that love is to be cultivated, and then given away totally and completely; that what we are is so much grander than the trivialities that often preoccupy us.

We are capable of so much more—capable of the kind of love that can mend what has broken and can change the course of history.

I want people to know that time is sacred and everyone has so very little of it here. We must be awake—to who and what we are, and to wake up to what we are capable of creating here on Earth.

We suffer because we have forgotten who and what we truly are.

We suffer because we cannot feel our glory. We suffer because we believe in the illusion of isolation and separateness. We suffer because of where and how we seek to remember.

Every place we look is an illusion—a false image of God. God cannot be found in money, in sex, in work, in accumulating material goods.

God can't even be found in the grandest temples, churches, and shrines. God is found within each of us—through a return to one's innate glory, beauty, and wisdom. That is where God lives—always. Not just during Sunday Mass, or in a meditation hall, or when kneeling to pray. God lives quietly in each of us illuminating the core of our being.

No god exists "out there" for us to find. Go inward, my friend. Search for the deepest center of your self, and there you will find me—right where I always am and have always been.

From your center, I look out, seeking you.

I am the "I" within you, whispering your name, stirring your longing, expressing the love you feel, see, and hear.

I am the Beloved.

We have important work to do together, you and I. I will guide you with my words, wisdom, vision, and knowing.

You will need to follow and implement. You are my face in public—one way the world can see me, one of the innumerable faces of God.

I must be your command tower now.

I must be the voice you listen to and follow.

I must be your source.

Turn your eyes and ears to me for your knowing.

I am the Source.

A few weeks later, I had another "meditation dialogue" with my soul.

"How are you today?" I asked.

I am so well. I'm delighted and thrilled you have finally found your way to me. I have waited for you for so long. Have you noticed how happy, peaceful, and calm you feel with my presence in your life? How much joy we have together?

Yesterday, you asked how deep I go. Well, I am deeper than the ocean and beyond the infinite cosmos. We are just beginning an endless exploration of this fascinating, wondrous universe. I will take you so many places.

Love is priceless. Continue to cultivate it—your deepest strength and core truth.

Don't ever be ashamed or embarrassed about your love, or the fact that you love. Let yourself love freely. Offer it with an open heart, without demand or expectation. Allow yourself to love because you can, because you must, because it's *you*.

The other day, you glimpsed that I am what others have always seen in you—the essence you have been unable to see and claim.

I am the gift that others experience you to be. I am your wisdom, beauty, and grace.

Finally, you have beheld me as yourself—the truest reflection of what you truly are.

We have time enough to spare, plenty for me to guide your life. No need, no urgency. Rest here.

Take comfort and solace and nourishment. Drink from the well that I am. I will always have enough to replenish you.

Allow yourself to stay open to gratitude—another expression of your essence. It opens and expands your heart, sweeping away bitterness and resentment. It forges a path to all that is holy, present and available. Continue to make space for me—for us. Wait and be patient, and I will speak. I will guide. I will know. And you/we will know.

Fierceness, too, has always been one of your greatest allies: fierceness to penetrate, fierceness to see, to know, to feel, fierceness to understand, to experience, and fierceness to give it all away.

That is your path. Follow it always. Give away everything you receive.

Eat it, imbibe it, digest it fully, then hand it over, and give it away.

Surrender every morsel and offer it as a blessing to the gods.

Pray as you take it all in. Pray as you digest it all. Pray as you offer it up. Make everything a sacred ritual. It always is.

Let every breath you take, and every step you make, be an act of prayer, ritual, love, devotion, celebration, and thanksgiving.

A few weeks later, I had another "soul dialogue"—perhaps one of the most poignant. I began by asking, "Okay, so, what's in there today?"

You're so funny. I'm beginning to feel performance anxiety!

I'm here. I'm not going to leave you. You can trust that. You can walk toward me, but you don't need to hunt me down. I'm right here. Always.

Sometimes I'll be quiet and still. No words, but I'm still here.

Sometimes I will be inspired and my words will gush forth like a mountain spring. Trust the ebb and flow. You have no reason to panic.

You are impatient; but I have existed for all time. Your life is but a blink of an eye. I existed long before you arrived, and I will continue to exist long after you go.

I am eternal and exist outside space. Distance means nothing to me. And I have all the time I ever need. No rush. No urgency.

I know you want to know what you should be doing with your life. Time will tell. I have no answer for you yet from the place of All-Knowing. So we wait. The cavern is deep and wide and an echo will rise up from the belly of the universe. Until then, you will not really know.

In the meantime, let your light and your love shine as you did yesterday. You laughed, you loved, you gave yourself fully away, and were in the play and *lila* of the moment.

Isn't that enough? Must you feel you have to leave your mark?

You want to do something, or be something, that will make you immortal—something to leave a lasting legacy.

But you already *are* immortal.

You really have nothing to prove. You already have your place in the cosmos. You deserve your space on planet Earth.

Human beings work so hard to prove themselves worthy. Pure folly!

That is why the Buddha laughs. It's hysterical, really.

The gods laugh at human folly. That's why the stars twinkle at night, as their bellies shake with laughter.

Seek nothing more than to remember. And once you do, then rest. Let this divine mystery play unfold before you, and watch with soft eyes.

The breezes at dawn have secrets to tell you
Don't go back to sleep!
You must ask for what you really want.
Don't go back to sleep!
People are going back and forth
across the doorsill where the two worlds touch,
The door is round and open
Don't go back to sleep!

— Rumi

CHAPTER 7

Aphrodite Awakens

AFTER TWENTY-THREE YEARS together, my husband and I decided to divorce. How does one unravel the many threads that lead to such a decision? For all those years, we had consciously used our marriage as our spiritual path. We had gone to couples therapy when we got stuck; we had tried to understand our childhood wounds and how we reenacted them with each other; and we tried to love each other as consciously as we were able.

However, Keith's habit of emotionally withdrawing triggered painful childhood memories and experiences of being abandoned by my mother. Every time he withdrew, I'd feel devastated, wounded, and abandoned all over again. I would then react by withdrawing to protect myself or lash out in anger. And so the cycle of childhood wounding would escalate: My anger reminded him of his emotionally distant mother and hostile father, which re-wounded him, and pushed him further away; naturally, this left me feeling even more abandoned.

During our years of counseling and therapy, we tried to learn how to talk through these moments with more openness, vulnerability, and accountability. We made heroic efforts to stop blaming each other, shared whatever we were feeling, and took the time to explain why. And for twenty-three years, those interventions worked. We kept digging more deeply into ourselves for better self-understanding, and this helped to enrich our intimacy and mutual appreciation, leading to deeper understanding and knowledge of ourselves and each other. We grew up together emotionally and helped each other to understand and heal much of our childhood trauma.

We also worked hard trying to overcome our sexual incompatibility. We tried Tantra and other sexuality-and-intimacy workshops, but never seemed to find a mutually satisfying sexual relationship. I felt frustrated by what I perceived as his lack of lust, passion, creativity and deep *emotional* presence. Early on in our relationship, I had felt shamed by what he deemed my "over sexuality." I felt judged and rejected and, as a result, I began to shut down sexually with him. Instinctively, I began to channel all of my "libido" into raising our children, as well as into the rewarding and demanding challenges of my career as a coach and seminar leader. Over time, we rarely made love and, when we did, it was mostly unsatisfying leaving me feeling even more alone.

During this time, my spiritual journey deepened and flourished. I taught workshops and seminars all over the world with the mystery school. I facilitated and guided participants in meditation retreats where they—and I—had many profound spiritual experiences. The Divine became my Beloved, replacing the relationship I missed in our marriage. My husband directed his libido into his business and career.

By the time our marriage ended, and despite our best efforts at therapy, we had grown in very different directions. He had spent most of our marriage building his business and career, while I dived deeper into my spiritual life. I hungered and ached for a rich spiritual, emotional, and sexual relationship with him, but our ships had set sail for different shores, and we could no longer find our way to each other.

Innocently enough, the beginning of the end happened for me one afternoon as I sat to eat my lunch and turned on an episode of *Oprah,* recorded on my Tivo. The show featured a makeover of a stay-at-home mom. I watched, engrossed, as the crew transformed a frumpy middle-aged housewife into a hot and sexy pole-dancer. Not only did they redo her hair, clothes, and makeup, they sent her to a pole-dancing class. I burst out crying. Sitting there, lunch half-eaten on my lap, I felt how my sexual passion had been deadened over the years of my marriage. I had sublimated my desire by focusing on my children and work, and I sobbed uncontrollably, as my sleeping inner Aphrodite roared awake after more than two decades of slumber. I grieved for all the lost vitality, juice, and creativity that had lain dormant in me all those years. At that moment, I vowed not to let her go back to sleep.

The *Oprah* show had impacted me so much that later the same day I tracked down a pole dancing class in my area, and immediately enrolled. The more I danced, the more I reconnected with my body and my sexuality. However, when I brought it home, my husband just didn't seem to know how to respond. With Aphrodite now fully reawakened in me, the emptiness of my sexual relationship with my husband stung even more—worse than with Aphrodite asleep. I did not want to let her go unconscious again, but I had no place to express her and satisfy my sexual desire. I was miserable.

That year, we went on vacation with another family to Hawaii. Our room wasn't ready when we arrived, so we went for a walk along the beach. We came across a man offering ten-minute chair massages, so I had one. I have had many massages over the years, and could tell this guy had good, strong hands. I got his card and arranged for him to come to our hotel room the next day to give me a full session—another nail in the coffin of my marriage.

While receiving massage, I often get sexually aroused. Fully relaxed and usually naked, when someone rubs my body it feels good, and my sexual desire awakens. As he worked on me, I silently wondered: "What would be the harm in him pleasuring me right now? He's touching every other part of my body, what is the artificial line here? Why can't he just bring me to an orgasm?" Without a word spoken between us, he must have intuited my desire, and began to pleasure me with his fingers. He brought me to . . . not one, not two . . . but *seven* orgasms on the massage table just with his fingers. After he left, I found myself sobbing yet again for what I was missing in my marriage. The session had fully reawakened my sexuality and I was determined not to let it go back underground.

I told Keith what had happened and expressed my grief over our sexual incompatibility. We promptly got ourselves back into couples counseling to try one more time to see if we could find our way to a mutually satisfying sexual relationship. We couldn't. Like oil and water, our incompatibility resisted all solutions. No amount of therapy, teaching, talking, or showing could get him to touch me the way my body liked.

Besides sexual satisfaction, I also hungered for a deeper emotional and spiritual connection. I knew that lovemaking with my Beloved could—and needed to be for me—a transcendent experience. Far beyond the goal of reaching an orgasm, spiritual lovemaking could, and would, transport both of us beyond, into something sacred. For me, lovemaking could be, and should be, an act of devotion and worship. I no longer wanted to separate my spiritual and sexual life. I wanted my love to be a state where all of my longing, devotion, and worship could be expressed and received by my Beloved. I wanted my sexual relationship to be sacred, reverential, and devotional. I longed to make love with my Beloved in a way that transported us. Keith and I simply could not ever find this kind of connection, despite how much we genuinely and deeply loved each other.

Still in analysis with my Jungian therapist, I anguished over these unmet longings. In order to fully express my desires, Seymour suggested I write out my sacred sexual fantasies in detail, focusing on the exact kind of sacred sexual encounter I longed for. I have decided to include below an explicit "fantasy scenario" that expresses my deep longing for a sacred, sexual, and devotional connection with a beloved at that time:

Tina's Eros: A Perfect Fantasy

You are expecting me when I arrive at your house around 10:00 AM. It's a beautiful sunny, breezy day. I am wearing a soft, cotton, flower-print dress in lavenders, greens, and blues—just sheer enough to show the outline of my naked body underneath. I ring the bell, and in less than a minute you open the door. You are wearing a pair of light tan pants, a brown belt, and a white shirt open at the collar. I can see your chest hairs peeking out slightly above the open collar. We greet each other with warm smiles and soft, penetrable eyes.

I lean upwards and gently kiss you, allowing my lips to lightly brush across yours. I feel my whole body begin to tingle, and I can sense the heat rising in you. You take my hand and lead me into the house. We are alone. The bright and airy room is filled with beautiful, fragrant red and pink roses. All the shades are up, and as I enter I can see out the windows to the stunning landscape, with two magnificent horses grazing in the meadow. The windows are open and I *sense* the land and the horses. My whole body feels alive.

As I gaze out the window, you move into the kitchen and begin packing us a picnic lunch and preparing ice tea. I stand beside you running my hand down the length of your arm, feeling the soft hairs as my palm glides over your warm, smooth skin. My body aches for you.

After a few moments, I remove my hand to pick up a cutting knife and begin dicing vegetables for our picnic. We stay there, in the kitchen, for about an hour, mostly in silence, standing side by side, preparing our food. I listen to your breathing and feel my breath beginning to move in rhythm with yours. The air is sweet. The only sounds breaking the silence are our breathing and the horses whinnying in the distance out the open window.

After packing for the picnic and gathering blankets, we move outside onto the porch and stop to take in the beauty of the scene. I am filled with gratitude for this moment: for the beauty of the land, the magnificent horses, and to feel you standing there beside me. My heart feels expansive in my chest and I breathe deeply and slowly.

You lead us to a place far off, on land sheltered by an enormous oak near a small river. We spread out our blankets and place the food in the shade. I turn to look at you and see you watching me, looking at my silhouette through my dress as the sun penetrates the cotton, illuminating my figure. I smile, as I look deep into your eyes. You smile, too.

I pull my dress up over my head, and let it fall beside me on the grass. Standing before you naked, I love the feel of the breeze against my skin. I begin to move, swaying with the breeze, like tree branches in the wind. I raise my arms above my head and begin to dance and twirl and bend and swirl. My whole body dances with the air. I feel the earth beneath my feet, supporting me with the mystery of gravity, while the heat of the sun penetrates my skin. Embraced by the vast, open, blue sky above us, I dance ecstatically. You sit on the blanket, watching me, beholding the splendor and enjoying the privilege of witnessing this extraordinary moment.

I dance and sing and laugh and cry and dance and laugh some more. You laugh and cry along with me. I turn to face you and, as I begin to approach, I slow down, locking my eyes on yours, until I am standing right in front of you. Then, playfully tantalizing, I lower myself and straddle you.

I remove your glasses, carefully placing them on the blanket beside you, and lightly kiss your forehead, closed eyelids, and the bridge of your nose. I lick away the tears drying on your cheeks, and then kiss you on the mouth. I run my fingers through your hair and I feel you surrendering to me—to my hands, to my mouth.

I explore your closed lips with my tongue as you open your mouth to welcome me. Playfully, I run my tongue along the inside and then the outside of your mouth. Your tongue finds mine, and they play together, performing their own dance. I hear you groan, and I wrap my arms tightly around you, pulling your body close into mine. After a moment, I lean back a little and caress your face with my right hand, gently gliding the tips of my fingers along your skin. I cradle your head in my hands and you exhale a full, deep, slow breath. For a timeless moment, we breathe together in silence, feeling the skin of our faces softly pressing against each other.

We sit together like that for a while, absorbing the sweet silence with our bodies. You stand up and take off your clothes, beginning with your shoes and socks, then your belt, pants, and underwear, and finally your shirt. You grab my hand, pull me up, and lead me into the pasture toward the horses. I follow behind so I can study you—your shoulders, your back, your ass, and your legs. I love looking at your body from behind as you lead me into the meadow.

As we approach the two grazing horses—a striking white mare and a magnificent chestnut stallion with a full, flowing black mane—you whistle a happy tune. I'm honored and delighted when you introduce me to these bold and majestic animals, and them to me. They interrupt munching the grass and raise their heads as you stroke their noses. They know you, and I can feel their love and trust for you and yours for them. You talk softly as you stroke and pat their shanks, showing me where and how they like to be touched. Sensing my interest, you tell me all about them—where they came from, how they came to you, and what they mean to you. I closely observe your strong hands as you stroke the mare and stallion— your long fingers caressing, loving, reassuring them.

We relish our time in the afternoon sun. I celebrate the pure joy of being with you and the horses, feeling the sun against my naked body and the sensuous warmth radiating off their animal bodies. I share your love for these beings, and I listen and watch attentively to how you affectionately interact with them. You help me appreciate their mystery and, through this, I can better appreciate the mystery of life.

As the sun begins to dip in the late afternoon sky, you lift me up with both hands and place me onto the stallion. You mount him behind me and, reaching from behind, grab the reins, gently pressing your feet into his sides until he begins to gallop. The mare runs freely beside us. I love the sensation of my hair blowing in the wind and my naked body bouncing against yours. The rhythm of the gallop between my legs excites me as we ride through the meadow. I am filled with the air, the sun, the land, the horses, and you.

Approaching our blankets in the shade of the oak tree, the stallion slows to a trot, and you release the reins. Reaching out from behind me, you take both of my breasts in your hands, as they bob up and down in rhythm with the horse. You gently nibble my neck and back, and this arouses me even more.

We slow to a stop, and the mare continues on down to the river to drink. You turn me around on the stallion to face you, my back toward his neck. You glide your fingers down my body, beginning at my lips, then my chin and neck, through my breasts, and down my belly. I lean back until I am pressed against the horse's neck, and then straddle my legs around your waist. With both hands, your long fingers stroke the front of my body ever-so lightly, and I feel goose bumps all over, even though the warm sun still caresses my body. I feel like a finely played instrument in the hands of a master musician.

You lean down into me and we kiss—slow, long, and deep. I feel the horse stir under us, as your tongue moves into my mouth, exploring. I reach my arms around you and knead and scratch your back. You like the sensation of my active fingers on your skin, warmed by the late-afternoon sun. You writhe in pleasure on top of me.

Time comes to a stop. We kiss and stroke each other. No hurry. Slowly, you sit up, grab my hands in yours, and pull me up to a sitting position so we face each other. Our eyes connect in silence, and we smile together.

You dismount first, lifting your right leg, swinging it over the horse, and slide off, until your feet touch the ground. You reach up to help me dismount, and I swing around to face you, then slide down the horse's warm flank into your arms. You pull me into you, and we stand face-to-face, naked bodies touching. I feel your hard lingam rising between my legs. I slide my hands down your back, grab your ass in my hands and squeeze both buttocks firmly. You groan and wriggle your cock against my body. I lean my head back and, opening my mouth slightly, sigh with pleasure as you kiss my neck and ears.

Still connected flesh-to-flesh, we stumble back to the blanket, and fall down laughing. Your eyes sparkle as we look into each other. With tender fingers, I trace the outlines of your mouth, nose, and eyelids, and stroke a lock of hair back off your forehead.

You roll onto your back and stretch out full-length before me. I move in close to kiss your body, beginning at your forehead, moving down your face, neck, and shoulders, across your chest, licking you and kissing you and stroking the hair on your chest with my fingers. You let yourself relax fully into the blanket, breathing in rhythm with my touches.

I move my mouth down along your thighs and you let your legs fall open. Your cock is hard and erect and resting against your belly. I continue kissing my way along your legs, over your calves and down to your feet and toes. I then begin to move my way back up your body, massaging and caressing your feet, calves, and thighs. Gently, yet firmly, I cup your balls in my left hand. You shiver and inhale quickly. I knead your balls with my fingers, expressing all of my love for you through my hand. I take the middle finger of my other hand and stroke it along the skin between your anus and scrotum. I caress the soft flesh around your balls and glide my fingers up and along your hard cock until I reach the tip of your penis. Straddling your legs, I grip your cock in my right hand and cup your balls in my left, as I stroke and knead. I lower my head, as if bowing to pray, to kiss and lick every millimeter of your lingam. I open my mouth and take your tip between my lips, then move my way down your shaft, still holding your balls in my left hand. You moan, moving your hips under me, and I feel your pleasure rising—exciting me even more. I run the fingers of my free hand along your belly, and gently comb and scratch through your chest hairs.

You lift your torso up toward me and roll me over onto my back. As you lean into me, I feel your cock gliding up my belly and between my breasts. You move up and down my body, rubbing your lingam against my mouth, breasts, and belly, and back again. I wrap my legs around your waist, pulling you closer. You massage my breasts and stomach with both hands, squeezing and kneading gently. As your hands cup and circle my breasts, your fingers find and tickle my nipples. I feel your cock graze across my vagina, driving my desire for you deeper.

You kiss my breasts, sucking, teasing, and tickling. We both laugh and giggle, enjoying the play of passion. You lick your way down between my breasts and over my belly, drawing circles with your tongue around my navel. When you insert your middle and ring fingers into my warm, wet yoni, I shudder and groan. You feel my insides welcoming you, wanting you. You trace your tongue around the lips of my yoni, probing, exploring, teasing. You suck and lick my clitoris, and push your fingers deeper inside me. I scratch your back and we both cry out with pleasure. I'm free-falling, opening and expanding and deepening all at the same time.

I grab you and pull you up to me, and we kiss. I taste myself on your mouth and feel my moisture all over your face. I lick your face and look into your eyes and smile. You smile back a wet, goofy, delirious smile, and we begin to laugh harder. As we laugh, I take your rock-hard, erect lingam and glide it slowly into my yoni. You hesitate with just the tip inside me, building our desire. Slowly, you push deep into me. I feel the muscles of my vagina giving way as your cock pushes past and through each layer of my flesh. I ache with desire to the depths of my body and being. You swivel your hips, bearing your weight down on me, and all I want is for you to keep going deeper. My hips begin to move with yours, and we rise and fall in unison. Our coupling is primitive and sacred. I look at the sky, the sun, the trees, the land, the horses—*you*. The beauty and perfection of the moment are almost more than I can bear.

An eagle flies above us, you pump faster and deeper into me, and as my hips rise to greet you, I scratch and laugh and cry in delight. I hear the eagle screeching, I hear you groaning, and I hear myself moaning as I feel you cumming inside me. You squeeze my ass tight as you are about to climax.

I allow the last layer in me to unfold and open, and everything in me explodes. I am convulsed by a tidal wave that begins deep within the center of my being and spreads out across the rest of my body in all directions sending tingles and shivers down my legs and arms and up my spine. I ride the wave of ecstasy. You take my face in your hands, and as we both climax together, your deep, soulful eyes pour right through me. We shudder and convulse, and scratch and grab each other. I can feel the folds deep within me contracting again and again around your pulsating cock. As the convulsing subsides, we hold each other tight. Both breathing slower now, I feel each part of your body relaxing, letting go. I release myself completely into you, and I begin to cry.

You kiss my tears as they roll down my cheeks. No words spoken, we lie there enveloped in a quiet, deep knowing. I trace your face gently with my fingers, and am surprised to find a tear there as well. You turn to kiss my fingers and I kiss your face. We lie there together in the dimming light, your now-soft cock still resting just inside me. The eagle flies in circles above us, and we smile. Savoring our wordless embrace, we softly stroke each other's bodies until we doze off peacefully in the warmth of the evening sun, caressed by the breeze. We share this moment of perfection with the horses and the eagle flying lazily above.

I awake to find you nuzzling and stroking the horses. I watch you without your knowing, delighting in the movements of your arms and hands—those strong hands that, just moments before, silently told me of your love and passion. I lie there, admiring your body and how it moves next to the horses. I close my eyes and feel immense gratitude for you, for this day, for this moment, for my life.

I sit up and prepare our picnic on the blanket. Accompanied by the horses, you amble over, and I offer you some grapes. You sit beside me, ravenously eating the fruit, as I feed some tender carrots to the hungry horses. We dine together—you, me, and the horses—until we are satiated. You lean back against the big, ancient oak and, spreading your legs, beckon me to sit against you. I lean back against your chest, you stroke my hair, and run your hands gently across my breasts. I stroke the hair on your forearms. Even though the sun is setting, the air is still warm and sweet.

We stay like this as the light gives way to night and the world turns to shadows. We talk about everything and nothing in particular, telling stories, and sitting together in quiet contemplation embraced by the still night air. We watch the stars slowly reveal themselves in the night sky, and I revel in the wonder of this moment. We lie there naked, taking in the majesty and mystery of life and all that surrounds us.

You stand, taking my hand in yours, pull me up and draw me close to you. Beneath the stars, we begin to dance slowly, our bodies pressed tight together. You sing softly in my ear and the sound of your voice soothes me. I welcome the warmth of your body against mine as the night begins to cool.

I've loved this day, and I feel gratitude as immense as the cosmos above. We dance and sing until fatigue drives us back to the blankets. Lying down again, I rest my head on your chest and curl my legs around yours. We wrap ourselves up in a warm blanket and lie there together staring up at the star-filled sky, feeling paradoxically insignificant and yet so full all at the same time. I feel us both slipping into the oceanic tides of slumber, and the last thing I remember is whispering into your ear some verses from Rumi:

Tina M. Benson M.A.

Out beyond ideas of wrongdoing and rightdoing, there is a field. I'll meet you there. When the soul lies down in that grass, the world is too full to talk about. Ideas, language, even the phrase "each other" doesn't make sense . . .

One day in couples therapy I finally blurted out: "I love this man. I have loved Keith for twenty-three years. I cannot imagine my life without him, and yet I cannot imagine my life with him anymore. I long to feel my sexuality joyously shared and fulfilled. I long for a deep spiritual and emotional connection that we just cannot seem to find with each other."

The tension in the room felt unbearable. My soul cried out in conflict: I honestly could not imagine my life without him after all those years, nor could I imagine feeling this unfulfilled for the next twenty-three years and beyond. I wanted more for myself and for him. We had always believed we would grow old together. Nobody stands at the altar on their wedding day expecting this moment to come. We had been the couple everyone believed in and looked up to. We had committed to a life together as two consciously, mutually loving partners, devoted to our marriage as a spiritual path. How, then, could we be yet one more statistic—part of the 51 per cent of marriages in the United States that end in divorce? We viewed our relationship as a beacon of hope to others.

Keith is a wonderful man, and I will always love him. We have two beautiful children, and had a spectacular home and loving life together. How do you justify walking away from all of that? With far less going for them, many people stay in marriages for lifetimes. And many women would have felt lucky and grateful for the husband, life, and home I had. I did, and do, feel fortunate, and will always feel gratitude for what we had.

So how does a deeper knowing, a deeper intuition, a deeper calling, a deeper insistence from the soul trump all of that? It just didn't make any sense to my rational mind. I had many reasons to stay—years spent building a life and family together, memories created together, many years of loving, learning, and growing together. And yet my soul cried out . . . I did not want to, and no longer could, live an unfulfilled life. Something deep within me wanted to be more fully alive, more joyfully and sacredly in union with my Beloved.

In my youth, sexuality had been primarily physical. However, following years of spiritual exploration, I was now much more adept at opening all the portals of my being. With deepening intimacy, I had learned to access the subtle realms where my "love-body" (as the great Indian mystic Ramakrishna called it) could travel. I knew how to let go, to draw my lover up and into specific experiential vortices, and I could express joy and ecstasy without any self-consciousness. None of that was easily available to me in my youth. Lovemaking had transformed into a devotional act, and I cherished the fact that I could now fully express *bhakti* in sexual union. I wanted lovemaking to be a playful, sacred, fun, juicy, creative, and heightened form of worship. Other than the trance states I enter when dancing, I know of no other greater joy.

After years of couples counseling, one day our therapist said something highly unusual—and memorable: "The two of you are just really different people. Clearly, you love each other, and you have certainly done years of work to learn how to communicate openly, honestly, vulnerably, and accountably with each other, and with love and admiration. There's really nothing I can do here. You're just two very different people; I can't change that."

And then he looked at me and said, "You are what Joseph Campbell would describe as being impaled on 'the horns of dilemma'."

"What?" I asked, trying to understand.

"When you're in a dilemma, there comes a time to eat the pear," he replied, cryptically.

"*What*?!" I said again, feeling more confused. "What the hell does that mean?"

"Well, you know, if you eat a pear too soon, it's not yet ripe, and if you eat a pear too late, it's overripe. There comes a point in a dilemma when it is time to eat the pear."

"Then, my prayer for myself is to know when it is time to eat the pear." And that's how the session ended.

That night, lying in bed, with Keith sleeping next to me, I was on fire with this dilemma. I really could not imagine my life without him, nor could I imagine staying with him any more. I could feel something pushing its way into my consciousness with an insistence that would simply no longer be denied. I felt certain I would go up in flames during the night, and that Keith would awaken to find nothing but a pile of ashes where I had slept. Eventually, I fell asleep.

Apparently something really did combust during the night because when I awoke and saw Keith lying there beside me, I *knew* the time to eat the pear had arrived. All the tension and angst, questioning and agonizing, doubting and uncertainty had disappeared. I looked at him sleeping there beside me and, with all of the love I had in my heart for this beautiful man, I knew our marriage was over. I felt certain and calm about this. During the night, something in the alchemy of sleep had sifted through all my ambivalent feelings, leaving me crystal clear. Although I loved this man with all my heart, and felt immense gratitude for our years together, the time had come for our marriage to end.

As it turned out, we had already arranged babysitting that night and were planning to go out to dinner and see a movie. As we got in the car, I took his hand in mine, looked at his handsome face, and declared: "It's time. Our marriage is complete, isn't it?"

"Yes, it is," he said with genuine love and gratitude.

We hugged each other and cried. Instead of going to a movie, we went to dinner and talked about how, when, and what our next steps would be. We laughed, we cried . . . we both felt relieved.

We decided to hold a marriage completion ritual to honor each other and our relationship. We took our wedding picture to the beach and spent an afternoon telling each other all we were grateful for, all we admired about each other, all we had learned from our time together, all we wished we had known to do differently, and about who we had become from loving and living as husband and wife. Consciously honoring each other and the life we had created together, we then released each other and our marriage— truly one of the most conscious, honoring, and loving ends to a marriage I know of.

Because we loved each other, because we didn't have a cataclysmic blow-up, because we had a beautiful home we both loved, and because our children still lived with us, we decided to continue living together as co-parents and roommates, sleeping in different bedrooms. This solution worked until we both started dating other people. A year after our "completion ritual," we decided to sell our home and move on to living separate lives.

Shortly after Keith and I decided to separate, I met a man with whom I shared a deep spiritual connection. Although we never consummated our relationship, during my time with him I experienced the deep emotional and spiritual bond I had longed for in my marriage—an affirming "wink" from the universe.

Stephen worked as a professional couples counselor, and we met over lunch to discuss his work. At one point in the restaurant, we lapsed into silence, and an unfathomable recognition filled the space between us—a meeting of souls that needed no language. I didn't think much more about it at the time, other than I felt I had just spent time with a lovely man, somebody I wanted to get to know more professionally.

We met again several weeks later to further discuss his couples work. Once again, almost as soon as I entered his home and sat down on the couch, we lapsed into an indescribable silent communion. From across the room, we gazed wordlessly into each other's eyes. Without speaking and without even touching, we made love to each other. Looking into his eyes, I felt I could fall all the way into an infinite universe residing just behind his eyes, and I *wanted* to. For more than two hours, I fell silently into his universe, and he into mine. Finally, he broke the silence: "You are such an invitation to fearlessness!" To this day, that remains one of the greatest compliments I have ever received. He then stood, walked over to me, bowed, kneeled, placed his head in my lap and breathed what felt like holy fire directly into by belly. His breath penetrated right down into the core of my being, reaching a lifetime's worth of longing and desire.

Unfortunately, because I was still living with my soon-to-be ex-husband, Stephen did not feel comfortable pursuing a relationship with me, concerned that Keith and I might resurrect our marriage. Nothing I said could persuade him that my marriage was over; that we had consciously ended it after many years of exploration and deliberation.

"You are everything I have ever wanted," he confided to me. "Being with you makes me happy. But I just can't be this close to the ending of your marriage."

I was devastated. I had just glimpsed what I had longed for, and now it had slipped through my fingers. I cried for months. I wrote him endless poetry and love letters, though I never sent them. Occasionally, I would email him when my longing became unbearable. Gracious and kind, and honoring his own sense of integrity, he remained unwilling to pursue a romantic relationship with me. By the time he finally did contact me, almost a year later, to say he felt enough time had gone by, and that he was now open to exploring a relationship, I had just begun my relationship with Pritam. Timing is so critical.

One evening, after Keith and I sold our house and had physically separated, I lay awake in the middle of the night, overcome with unbearable longing. I had left my marriage hoping for a deep, spiritual, emotional, sexual union with a beloved. I had soon met Stephen with whom that had been a real possibility, but because I still shared a home with Keith, he chose not to get involved. I lay there, wide awake at 2:00 AM, burning with desire, wondering, "Where is my Beloved? "Is he out there? Will I ever find him?" And then I had a sudden inspiration: I decided that, until or unless the glorious day came when "*he*" came into my life, I could still have the relationship with a Beloved that I longed for.

I devised a plan to send an email to my unknown Beloved—using my own email address. When the message arrived in my inbox, I would reply to my Beloved (same email address), thus making me both the Beloved and the Loved— the one longing and the one being longed for. I would continue to send these letters to myself until another Beloved appeared in my life. In the meantime, at least I could engage in the act and experience of being Lover and Beloved.

I wrote a beautiful "love letter" to my unknown Beloved, pouring out my heart and soul's yearning, longing, and desire.

I filled it with poetry and romance, and emailed it to myself. The next day I left for a prearranged camping trip with my daughter and friends. When I got home several days later, the email was there, waiting for me in my inbox. Amazingly, the email right above it had come from Pritam, the man I had met in India six months earlier. I didn't know it at the time, but my letter of longing for a Beloved—sent out "blindly" to the universe—had miraculously been answered by an actual, real Beloved! Although I didn't know it at the time, Pritam would change my life forever—in ways I could never have anticipated.

CHAPTER 8

India Calling

WHEN SHE IS ready to receive you, and you are ready to receive her, India comes calling—that's how it was with me. My love affair with India began many years before I first traveled there in 2006. As a student of the world's major religions, I found myself drawn to Eastern spiritual traditions, especially Hinduism, Buddhism, and Sufism. With two children at home, I did not imagine I would travel to India until they were both grown and out on their own. However, India has a way of conspiring when it is time.

In 2006, I visited my dear friend and colleague Jodi, who was leading a meditation retreat in Paulden, Arizona. We spent three days together at the Miraval Spa while the retreatants took the time to practice silence and fasting. Sitting poolside, she talked about how she longed to return to India. I told her how much I'd love to join her, but with two children at home, I didn't see how it would be possible for another ten years or so. Nevertheless, we began to fantasize about our ideal trip and what we both felt we *had* to see. By the time I left Arizona, we had planned our itinerary and I went home determined to see if my husband would support this "wild" idea.

To my surprise, he agreed because he could see how deeply I felt India was calling me. We decided to get support for him with the kids, and I immediately began to plan a trip with my friend. We outlined our entire itinerary, scheduled dates, and set the wheels in motion. While I had two kids at home, Jodi was in the middle of an adoption process. A few months before the start of our trip, she had to bow out. Unfortunately, the timing clashed with adoption agency visits to the home she shared with her partner. Instead of heading off on our journey to the East, Jodi prepared for her own new adventure with their soon-to-be daughter.

Faced with the dilemma of deciding whether to go to India alone or cancel this trip altogether and wait for another time when she could join me, I listened to my heart . . . it was already there: My dreams already danced with images of traveling through India; I already had my husband's full support; we had already asked his mother to come stay with him and the kids for the three-and-a-half weeks I would be gone. The prospect of traveling alone for the first time in India seemed daunting, even risky. Then a miraculous synchronicity happened.

I was at the California Institute of Integral Studies (CIIS), in San Francisco, to attend a lecture by my ecstatic dance teacher, and saw a brochure promoting continuing education courses. Waiting for the lecture to begin, I absentmindedly opened the brochure to a page describing an upcoming trip to India as one of their extension courses. Unbelievably, the itinerary for the trip was almost exactly what my friend and I had planned, and very close to the dates we had chosen. I decided then and there to go, and registered the next day. Within a week, I had enlisted two girlfriends to join me, and the trip was set.

In December 2006, we boarded a San Francisco flight bound for Delhi, with several CIIS faculty and other participants. I had no idea that my life was about to change forever. The moment the plane landed on India soil, I felt I had come home. My soul resonated deeply to the cacophony of sights, sounds, and smells. People have said you either love India or you hate it; there really isn't anything in between. On arrival, an onslaught of sensory stimuli greets you—an invisibly organized chaos, orchestrated to a kaleidoscope of images and sounds. You either surrender to India on its terms and go with the flow, or risk crazy-making overwhelm if you fight the chaos. Sustained resistance is not really an option when surrounded by hundreds of millions of people who live differently. Resistance leads to an abrasive experience that can rapidly shred your nerves. I surrendered immediately.

We flew from Delhi to Chennai and then made our way to the ashram of one of India's great saints, Sri Aurobindo, in Pondicherry, South India. Sri Aurobindo was an extraordinary scholar, lawyer, and spiritual leader who, together with his spiritual partner, The Mother, created a radically innovative spiritual community called Auroville. Aurobindo and The Mother aimed to establish an international community, inside India, but beyond Indian governance; a community that could live peaceably and democratically, honoring all faiths and practicing Aurobindo's philosophies.

I spent my first night in India at Auroville, and stayed for a week exploring southern India. We visited extraordinary temples in Chidambaram and Mahalamapuram. We also walked the old streets of Pondicherry, a former French enclave in colonial days. Architecturally, Pondicherry is more like New Orleans than India.

On New Year's Day 2007, we saw an epic rendering of the *Mahabharata*, one of India's great spiritual stories, set against the backdrop of the Mahalamapurum caves. In 2004, when the ocean briefly receded during the great tsunami that devastated so much of Indonesia, an entire underwater temple complex, hidden for centuries undersea, was discovered at Mahalamapuram.

The previous night in Auroville, I "knew" my marriage was about to end. Our group had gone to the Tibet House for their annual New Year's Eve meditation in an enormous hall with thousands sitting in concentric circles, as well as people hanging out up in the rafters. The setting was truly spectacular, lit with thousands of flickering candles. As 2006 turned into 2007, I was deep in meditation, thinking about nothing in particular at that moment, when I heard a voice inside my head say, "Your marriage is going to end." Although Keith and I were struggling to find ways to deepen our intimacy, we were still deeply committed to our marriage, and so I disregarded the voice and went on with my meditation—but it kept nagging at me.

Next, our group traveled from southern India to Jaipur and then on to Agra to see the Taj Mahal and surrounding forts and temples. The Taj Mahal is indescribable; its majesty, beauty, and scale truly incomprehensible. We then traveled to Delhi where we visited the site of Gandhi's murder and last speech, as well as the *ghat* along the Ganges where his ashes were taken, Muslim mosques, Hare Krishna temples, and Hindu temples and shrines. Then we traveled to the most sacred Hindu city of all, Varanasi. This is the "Mecca" for Hindus from all over the world. It is considered very auspicious to have your cremation on the banks of the Ganges in Varanasi and to have your ashes given to Mother Ganga.

I have no words to describe the chaos that is India, much less Varanasi. It is one of the most congested cities in the world. All manner of vehicles, cars, buses, bicycles, rickshaws, pedestrians, cows, sheep, children, chickens, loin-cloth-clad *sadhus*, foreigners, pilgrims, devotees, all share the patchwork of roads. No designated "lanes" of any kind exist, and traffic seems to move in every direction all at once. We settled into our hotel in the "Cantonment" section of town and then took rickshaw rides through the thick of humanity. I couldn't have been happier. I was thrilled by the chaos of it all. One of the faculty members in our group was so traumatized, she took to her bed for the next two days. I, on the other hand, felt completely at home.

The next day, we took a boat ride along the Ganges at sunset to where the evening *"aarti"* is performed. This sacred sunset ritual has been enacted by Hindus each evening along the Ganges for thousands of years. It is their way of putting the river to sleep each night. Thousands of Hindu pilgrims and foreigners descend upon the *ghats* (steps down to the water) at the riverbank, light candles, and send their prayers into the river. For the Hindus, Mother Ganga (as they call the river) moves through their world as a living presence, a sacred being to which prayers and offerings are made.

As we approached the main *ghat* from our boat, thousands of people lined the steps and the riverbank, sitting and waiting for the evening *aarti* to begin. Seven large platforms held seven Brahmin priests. I could hear bells clanging, and the scent of incense filled the air, adding to the sense of anticipation.

The ritual began with a special ringing of the bells, followed by an hour-long, synchronized ritual performed by the seven Brahmins. As I watched from the boat, I spontaneously entered a trance-like state and began to perform the exact movements of the ritual in perfect synchronization with the Brahmins. Having never seen or witnessed these rituals before, I am at a loss to explain how my body knew the movements and was able to perform the rituals. At the end of the *aarti*, when we disembarked from the boat and my feet touched down for the first time on the banks of the Ganges in Varanasi, I burst out crying—my natural response to a profound feeling of coming home. Thankfully, my tour guide and now dear friend, Richard, who, unknown to me, had had a similar experience his first time in Varanasi, came over and held me while I wept. He then took me to a nearby Brahmin priest who walked me into the Ganges and performed a ritual with me. In a deliriously blissful state, I felt I had returned home after lifetimes of wandering.

When the tour ended, I stayed on in India with a friend because I still *needed* to see two more places: Mother Theresa's orphanage and her Samadhi Shrine in Calcutta, and the Khajuraho Temple complex. Before traveling on to Calcutta, we stayed a few extra days in Varanasi, and became friends with a local shopkeeper named Baboo, who decided to be our personal host. He took us for rides along the Ganges in his boat, took us for meals in his friends' restaurants, piled us high with *saris*, Indian bedspreads, and altar cloths, and took us to meet his astrologer Brahmin priest. Based on his reading of my astrological chart, and with no mention of my New Year's Eve meditation warning, the priest told me my marriage would be ending. He also told me I had lived at least six prior lives and that in my immediate previous lifetime I had been a priestess but had misused my power. He stated that this was to be my last life because, this time, I would embody the Priestess archetype and finally master my relationship with power. I didn't quite know what to make of everything he said, but, one more time, the message that my marriage would be coming to an end rang loud and clear.

From Varanasi, we traveled to Calcutta. All my life, I have been inspired by Mother Teresa. Had I not been born in Los Angeles in the1960s in a non-practicing Jewish home, but rather in a small Catholic village somewhere in Europe, I might very well have followed her path into the nunnery. I have always felt a very deep calling to live a life of service and devotion. Because Mother Teresa has been such a personal heroine of mine, I felt deeply called to make a pilgrimage to

Calcutta, to visit the Samadhi Shrine where she is interred, and to spend a day doing *seva* (service) at one of her Calcutta orphanages.

Calcutta really is the poorest of the poor. Begging, limbless children fill the streets, and homeless shanties and slums litter the landscape—yet a raw beauty shines from it all. We wandered our way past a begging limbless man lying on the street, and eventually found our way to her main orphanage. We spent a day there playing with the children, and my heart broke for each of them. I wanted to adopt and rescue them all, and bring them back with me to the U.S. where they would surely have a better future. The nuns who devote their lives to these beautiful children were so loving and kind, and the faces and hearts of the children were so open. Their faces still haunt me today.

Next, we made our way to Mother Teresa's Samadhi Shrine, a humble resting place for such a heroic woman and saint. In a small room, I sat in meditation before her marble casket adorned with flowers. I felt immense gratitude for the life she had chosen—in service to countless numbers of children whose leprosy-filled bodies she had lovingly touched and caressed. I poured my gratitude directly from my heart into her casket.

Calcutta had other remarkable moments, among them the main Kali temple. Known in Hinduism as the consort of Shiva, the black goddess Kali, represents *shakti* (sacred empowerment), time and change. Well, my friend and I, two white American women, had no idea what we were in for! As we entered the temple compound, our bare feet were met with a combination of filth and animal blood. Wading through the thick sludge, we came across animal sacrifices in progress, including beheading of chickens. Until that moment, I didn't know that a headless chicken will run around spurting blood from its neck for quite some time. Most definitely, we were not in Kansas anymore!

In Calcutta, a lovely Muslim man, who had been our cab driver, befriended us and invited us to visit his family's mosque. Women are not typically let into mosques during prayer time, but he snuck us in through a back door, and spirited us up to the top level where we could watch the evening prayers below. At the appointed time, a *muezzin* call resounded from the speakers, and thousands of men poured in, knelt upon the small prayer rugs, turned to face Mecca, and began their evening prayers. I knew that I was witnessing a side of these men that many of their own wives, mothers, and daughters would never see. Muslim men are often quite stoic publicly, but here thousands of them prostrated low on their knees praying, some weeping, and I felt deep gratitude to have witnessed this most sacred and private moment in these men's lives.

After Calcutta, we journeyed by train to Khajuraho to see the temple complex —where ancient sacred *tantra* rites and rituals had been performed, and where the text of the epic *Kama Sutra* is carved into the stones. I had to see this. The temples had been lost for centuries, overgrown by jungle, until the colonial British stumbled upon them in the late 1800s and dug them out. Now a world heritage site, the temples are no longer places of active worship.

I have been a dancer for most of my life, having studied modern and jazz dance throughout high school and college, but in later years gravitated more toward unstructured ecstatic trance dancing. For years, I would often enter deep trance-like states as I danced. In these states, my body would begin performing specific *mudras* (symbolic hand gestures used in Indian dance and Hindu and Buddhist ceremonies, and often depicted in statuary and paintings). I had no idea where my spontaneous *mudras* came from, but I felt they belonged to some temple where these specific dances had been performed. I have always felt myself to be a temple dancer, and suspected that these *mudras* might have belonged to the dances and temple rituals that took place in Khajuraho.

Within minutes of entering the first temple, I immediately found myself in a deep trance. I stood in meditation, and began to experience clear and detailed sounds and images flooding my awareness. I felt as if I was being transported through time and space and could see and hear the worship that had taken place in these temples during sacred rituals. I could see the temple dancers and hear the music. I also saw that these were the *very* dances and *mudras* I had spontaneously performed during my earlier ecstatic trance dances. Again, I have no way of explaining how my body knew these *mudras* or dances, but if there is such a thing as past lives, I've no doubt that I was most definitely a Khajuraho temple dancer, devoted to ancient and sacred Hindu *tantric* worship and practices. Later research did, in fact, confirm that the music I had heard in my meditation, and the dances I had seen in my meditation were the exact practices, dances, and rituals that had taken place in those temples hundreds of years ago.

I have seen this type of thing happen many times in the meditation retreats I have taught over the years. Once, in a two-week retreat, a woman who had just emerged from a very deep meditation stood up and began writing very complicated metaphysical equations on a large piece of paper fixed to the wall. She had absolutely no idea how she knew what to write, and only by sheer coincidence a metaphysical scholar happened to be present who was able to confirm the accuracy of her calculations! I have seen this so often over the years, I completely trust that, when we enter deep states of meditation, we have access to infinite sources of knowledge and wisdom. Some wisdom traditions suggest that the *akashic* records (the cosmic database of every experience and event that has ever happened, by whom and to whom) are available to all of us in meditative states. At any rate, my body did know these ancient temple dances, and, unwittingly, I had been performing them for years.

As soon as I got home from that first trip to India, I decided to return again the following year. Just a few months after we were back in the States, Richard, our CIIS tour guide, hosted a faculty luncheon and invited some of us who had been on the trip to talk about our experience. After lunch, Richard and I went for a walk and discussed my organizing another tour group to India—I wanted to take a group the next year. As it happened, I met another CIIS faculty member who was organizing the World Congress on Psychology and Spirituality in Delhi the following year, 2008. I told him about research I had been doing on comparative religions, and he invited me to present my findings at the conference. I needed no other reason to go: I would give a presentation at the Delhi conference and afterwards lead a tour group through India.

During my first CIIS India tour, I had befriended our tour guide, Ratan, in Varanasi. He and I had spent countless hours talking together on long bus rides and I had gotten to know a lot about him and his family. When my girlfriend and I had stayed on after the rest of the CIIS group had left, Ratan invited us to his home, introduced us to his wife and children, cooked us a delicious traditional Indian meal, hired exquisite musicians to play music for us, and treated us like royalty. He had even managed to persuade his very shy, non-English speaking wife to drag out her wedding sari to show us. By the time I left, I felt a deep connection with Ratan and his family.

As I planned my next tour to India, without hesitation I contacted Ratan and asked him to be my personal guide for the trip. He was delighted, and together we began to craft our itinerary. However, just a few months before the trip, I received an email from his son, Arpit, informing me that Ratan had suddenly and unexpectedly died of a massive heart attack followed by a brain hemorrhage. I was devastated, shocked and stunned, and grief-stricken, and promised his son I would visit his family again when I returned to India the following year.

I scrambled to reorganize the tour with another travel agency, and managed to fill it. In January 2008, I returned to India with my new group and to present at the conference in Delhi—one of the highlights of my life.

My research project was originally prompted by the horrific events in New York on September 11, 2001. Along with millions around the world, I sat in horror as I watched unthinkable images of the attack on the World Trade Center towers. I struggled to comprehend what had happened and why, and how were we, as humanity, supposed to respond?

As I sat in my counseling office listening to the grief of my clients, and feeling my own hopelessness and despair as the U.S. government seized the opportunity to create a global war-based campaign of "good guys vs. bad guys," "us vs. them," I asked myself, "What can I, one person, do to combat this dangerous polarizing consciousness?" I imagined and believed that, at our core, human beings—no matter where we live, no matter what God we pray to, or even whether or not we pray at all—are fundamentally more alike than different. If I could amass a body of interviews of people answering one question—*"In the deepest part of your soul, what really most matters to you?"*—and get the data out to the public, I might be able to help turn the tide to reverse the polarizing consciousness my government was determined to put in place. At the very least, I could attempt to create a different conversation.

As part of my research, I asked anyone I could to allow me to interview them and respond to that one question.

Initially, I believed we would all essentially end up saying the same thing—and this proved to be true. However, I was surprised by *what* we all ended up saying. Essentially, each interviewee said that, at our core, we all carry some kind of cellular memory of a time when we were joined in union with Source/God/Soul/Essence/Presence—a time of no-separation from something bigger than ourselves; a time when we knew ourselves to be *one* with everything and everyone. We all possess a deep fundamental longing to return to that knowing of our original *oneness*. This is the deepest impulse behind all human action.

My research data left me with broader questions about their implications for social, environmental, political, and economic domains. If we are driven by a deep yearning to remember we are one with Source, how might this knowledge affect policy making, environmental decision-making, even marketing and advertising? How might it impact international relations? Without "us vs. them," or a sense of separation between humans and the rest of nature, we would no longer hurt our neighbors, kill enemies, or rape the planet. How could we—once we recognize we really are all one?

I had originally intended to transcribe the interviews into a book, but with just months before my trip to the World Congress in India, I decided instead to create a film—*What Matters Most*—a more visually creative way to present my research. I spliced together sound bites from the interviews with images of people in different forms of prayer and worship around the world. It is a beautiful film and I feel quite proud of it.

And so, in January 2008, I stood in front of a large audience in Delhi, as my movie debuted on two enormous screens. It was thrilling, and I was humbled to see how many people were moved to tears by the combination of voices and images. After the Q & A, a throng swarmed around me to personally tell me how the film had touched them. My little movie has since been shown around the world in places as far flung as Barcelona, Uzbekistan, Britain, New Zealand, Portugal, and Bali, and has even become part of a public school curriculum in London and New Zealand.

After the World Congress, my group and I moved on to touring various sacred sites in India. We traveled throughout Delhi; visited the Taj Mahal in Agra; traveled to the Allora and Adjanta caves in Aurangabad, an amazing complex of cave carvings dating back to second century BCE; we journeyed to Mumbai; and to the exquisite southern beaches of Goa.

When we arrived back in Varanasi, I kept my promise to visit Ratan's widow and children. At his home, we were greeted in much the same way my friend and I had been received the previous year. A delicious and abundant meal had been prepared for all of us, only this time the household was filled with grief and loss. Ratan's devastated wife, who had been unable to leave her bedroom for months and whose wails of grief filled the home, was barely able to visit with us. I asked if I could see her privately in her bedroom, and as I sat with her on her bed, she sobbed in my arms and my heart broke for her despair and loss. To be a widow in India is a helpless and hopeless situation. What I didn't know at the time was that Ratan was the only provider for the entire extended family of 20-plus people who lived with him. Because he spoke English and German, he had a means of supporting all of them by being a tour guide.

When I asked his widow what I could do to help, her main concern was for her children and that they be able to finish their education, as Ratan had deeply wished for them. Without an education in India, there is little hope of avoiding permanent abject poverty. At that moment, I vowed to myself to do whatever I could to help support Ratan's three beautiful children complete their education. Back home from my trip, I sent an email out to all of my family and friends and raised enough money to keep the children in school. So many people around the world need help, I never know where to begin. In this case, however, I had a personal connection, and it mattered to me that Ratan's kids have a chance to make it.

Next stop on our itinerary after visiting Ratan's family, I had planned to take the group to the main Hindu temple in Varanasi. However, when we arrived at the temple large signs declared: "NO NON-HINDU ENTRY ALLOWED." Armed guards patrolled the perimeter to enforce the prohibition. I tried negotiating, bargaining, flirting, even bribing the guards to let us in, but they had none of it. The group gave up and walked on down the street to do some shopping. An inexplicable longing and need to be inside the temple seized me. I tried over and over to persuade the guards, but to no avail. I decided to just stand in front of the temple doorway and say, "*yes*" to my longing, whether or not I could have what I wanted.

Months had passed, and I still pined for Stephen, the man with whom I had had that deep spiritual connection just after my husband and I had separated. My heart was full of longing for things and people it seemed I couldn't have. I stood in front of that temple doorway, closed my eyes, and breathed even more desire into my longing. Everything in me wanted to get inside. In that moment, I realized that although I might never be in control of getting what I longed for, I could always say "yes" to my own longing. I surrendered to my longing and to the outcome.

I honestly don't know how long I stood before that doorway with my eyes closed; I lost all sense of time and space. At some point, I felt somebody touch my shoulder, and when I opened my eyes, I was astonished to see one of the armed guards and the temple priest. Seeing my profound longing, the guard had apparently gone inside, told the temple priest about this crazy American woman standing outside, and together they had come to get me. The next thing I knew, the temple priest was helping me across the threshold of the temple and into the inner sanctum where I promptly fell to the ground sobbing in tears of gratitude. It was a seminal moment in my life: I learned yet again that, regardless of circumstances, my job is to say, "yes" to my own longing . . . the rest I surrender to the universe.

I didn't know it at the time, but at the Delhi World Congress, I had met the man who was to become my next lover and partner. Because Pritam was Indian and had a home in India, over the next three-and-a-half years, I traveled many times to visit him there. We took many visits to Sai Baba's ashram in Puttaparthi, where my Indian lover had his home. Although Sai Baba had not been my personal guru, many experiences at his ashram had touched me deeply. Sai Baba died in April 2011, a few months after my last visit there. I was grateful I had journeyed there with my children and that they had had a chance to see him. On Christmas Eve 2010, I sat in the first row of Sai Baba's enormous ashram, and wept with gratitude as he was pushed past us in his wheelchair. He took a moment to pause and look at my daughter, Maya. I don't know what her young nine-year-old psyche made of the spectacle, but it moved me deeply to see her there.

Over the years, Pritam and I traveled throughout the sub-continent visiting Bangalore, Mysore, Cochin, and Delhi to see his colleagues and friends. In the summer of 2010, we decided to undertake an arduous journey to do the Chardham Yatra pilgrimage in the Himalayas. Chardham is one of the most renowned and holy expeditions in India, and includes visits to four sacred shrines including Yamunotri, Gangotri, Kedarnath, and the Badrinath Dham. Because of time constraints, we decided to forego Yamunotri.

We flew from San Francisco and spent a few days in Delhi visiting friends, and then traveled to Rishikesh—the yoga hub along the banks of the Ganges at the foothills of the

Himalayas, made famous by the Beatles when they traveled there in the 1960s with their guru Maharishi Mahesh Yogi.

In Rishikesh, we stayed at an ashram that held special significance for Pritam, as this was one of the places he had visited soon after his wife had died, and where he had sprinkled her ashes into the Ganges. A friend of mine from the States, had also arrived in Rishikesh, so we invited him to join us at the ashram for a day of touring and to perform a ritual at the riverbank in honor of Pritam's late wife. As soon as my friend arrived at the ashram, Pritam reacted, and things became tense between us. Although he had invited my friend to join us for the ritual, and to stay on at the ashram and tour the neighboring surrounds, Pritam became very jealous. I offered to sit in the front of the car with the driver so Pritam could sit in the back with my friend and they could get to know each other, he declined. But then he became suspicious that my friend and I were "making out" in the back seat. Unfortunately, this was one more example of the crazy suspicions and paranoias that had plagued our relationship from my very first visit to India with him more than two years before. We had horrendous arguments in Rishikesh, and, again, nothing I could say or do would persuade him nothing salacious was happening with my very-married friend.

Nevertheless, despite the tension and discord, we soldiered on up the Himalayas. Traveling to do the Chardham Yatra is an arduous journey to say the least. To get to each of the Gangotri and Badrinath temples requires a ten-hour drive up steep one-lane, badly paved roads, alongside sheer cliff drops down to the river below. Without passing lanes, you share the road with cars, trucks, buses, cows, sheep, motorcycles, and barefooted *sadhus* making their way up and down the mountain. Every year, many cars plunge over the mountainside, killing hundreds. The dangers and perils are real, and you feel it every kilometer up and down the mountain as you stare off into the abyss at your side.

Getting to the Kedernath temple had its own unique peril: The only way to get there is to drive half way up the mountain and then either ride donkeys for an additional eight-hour ride, walk the mountain for a several-day journey, or take a helicopter ride through the narrow and steep Himalayan passages. To save time, we opted for the harrowing helicopter ride. They could accommodate only one passenger at a time, so I went first, by myself, up into the fog and mists of the Himalayas, saying a silent but very fervent prayer to myself that I would live to see my children again.

Our itinerary took us first to visit Gongotri, a beautiful temple nestled right alongside the frigid northern waters of the Ganges, close to its source in the Himalayas. We performed a ritual by the river with a temple priest, where I prayed that the torment in my Indian love's soul would be healed and that he would come to trust and rest in my love for him. I lit a candle and sent my prayers into the river as I stood knee-deep in the freezing water.

From Gongotri, we traveled down the mountain and then, next day, across the mid-section of the mountain, before going back up the mountain to the helicopter pad for our trip to Kedernath. Having survived our helicopter rides, we celebrated arriving at our hotel. Kedernath had deep personal meaning for Pritam: Shankaracharya, a guru and saint, is believed to have lived and attained his final *samadhi* there—a holy site marked by his "Samadhi Shrine." Pritam believed himself to be a reincarnation of Adi Shankara, a Vedic philosopher in the early eighth century CE.

After resting in our hotel room, we walked the path up to the temple, which was closed until later that evening. Walking further along, we found our way to Shankaracharya's shrine. As we entered the building, the fog and mist outside were so thick it was impossible to see where we were in relation to the surrounding mountains. Inside the cavernous room, at the very far end several life-size marble deities surrounded a marble casket.

I immediately entered a trance state. Pritam walked toward the base of the shrine and collapsed into a fetal position on the floor. To our great surprise, we had the place all to ourselves for the next three hours. I felt compelled to circumambulate the shrine as Pritam remained in a fetal position on the floor. I moved around it seven times, and then walked back near the entrance of the building and sat against the wall keeping vigil.

As I sat there watching Pritam crumpled on the floor against Shankaracharya's shrine, my heart burst wide open. I was overcome with an enormous sense of compassion for his tortured and tormented soul. I can't claim to know if, in fact, he is a reincarnation of Shankaracharya, but I know his soul never wanted to incarnate into a human body in this lifetime. He has an otherworldly cerebral mind, making him a supremely rarified intellect that has little-to-no capacity for ordinary human engagement. He thrives in the ivory towers of academia where the mind reigns supreme, but here on the Earth's platform, in the realm of human feelings, interactions, and discourse, he was woefully inept and he knew it. He felt like an alien and called himself one often.

I sat there, my heart overflowing with empathy and compassion for his torment, and could feel him traveling back to the eighth century CE, imploring the Gods, "Why do I have to exist in this human body? I can't do it. I don't know how." And as he lay there crumpled, I journeyed with him back through time, and could feel all the ways that this human embodiment had tortured and tormented him. I could feel how utterly lost he was, and my heart wept for him.

For more than two hours, I sat holding this openhearted vigil for him until he eventually stood up, walked over to me, and crumpled into my arms on the floor where he sobbed and wailed and moaned. All I could do was hold him while he wailed. It was a primitive, anguished, and tortured crying, as if the entire injustice of his incarnation were being grieved. Not a word was spoken between us. When he was finished crying, we stood up. He was wobbly on his feet, and his eyes told me he was not totally in his body. He had traveled somewhere and had not yet fully returned. I steadied him with my hand on his back, and when we walked back outside the door, the fog and mist had miraculously lifted, revealing that we were right up against the most magnificent snow-capped peaks of the Himalayas. Not just the literal fog and mist had lifted, but the psychic fog as well. With my hand steadying his back, I guided him back to our room where I held him throughout the night. We never talked about what had happened at the shrine; we didn't need to. We both understood, and he was grateful I had held him through that nightmarish process.

The next day, after an eight-hour delay due to fog, we took a helicopter ride back down to our car and, having driven back down the mountain, we were on our way to Badrinath—our last shrine visit on the Chardham Yatra. On the trip, we encountered heavy early monsoon-like rains. All of a sudden, dozens of rain-soaked men ran up towards us screaming that the road ahead had just washed out. A truck had careened over the cliff just a few yards ahead of us, killing the driver. We had nowhere to go. Serendipitously, this happened just in front of the only "hotel" for many kilometers. Because we were the first car to reach the washed-out road, we were one of a fortunate few to get a room for the night. By the time we woke in the morning, a long line of cars trailed behind us for miles, with people sleeping in their cars and on the roofs of their cars without food or shelter, in the pouring rain. Nobody knew how long it would take to repair the road, so we hunkered down in our meager accommodations, considering ourselves to be the lucky ones. Had we been just a few kilometers ahead, it could easily have been us who had careened over the mountain's edge.

By noon the next day, the road was repaired, and we were on our way again to Badrinath, where another amazing India experience awaited us. Badrinath is situated way up in the northernmost tip of the Himalayas, bordering Tibet and China. The Mongolian/Tibet influence is visible in the different architecture of the main temple and in the faces of the residents in the neighboring town of Mana. Walking up the mountain past the temple into the little town of Mana, we stumbled upon a village gathering where we witnessed possession rituals. The assembled crowd would begin to chant and one or two people at a time would begin to spin until the "possession" took place. Then, the elders would gather around, providing a sacred boundary, while this person swung himself wildly around in some kind of ecstatic frenzy. These things can seem strange to Westerners, but altered states of consciousness are not only understood in these other cultures, they are also encouraged and revered. By entering trance states, they can access spirit worlds in ways Western culture no longer can.

After visiting the main Badrinath temple, the next day we decided to hike further up the mountain. On our way up, we encountered a *sadhu*, or holy man, living inside a little cave in the mountainside—literally no bigger than the inside of my Prius. As if inviting us into a royal palace, he proudly ushered us inside. We literally had to get down on our hands and knees to crawl inside the tiny opening. I was astonished to see how, in such a tiny space, he had managed to create a home—with a sleeping space, a small cooking area, and a sacred altar. All of his worldly possessions were here inside this little cave. He lived there year round, completely snow-bound for nine-plus months, rarely seeing people. We were one of a few who had ever ventured beyond the temple and further up the mountain. With the generosity of a king, he cooked *chapattis* and *chai* tea for us, and insisted we sit, eat, and rest. I sat there, in his humble abode, thinking about my four-bedroom home back in California with all of my "stuff," and envied him the simplicity of his life; but mostly I was deeply moved by his generosity. He had very little to give, but what he did have, he offered to us. I will never forget him.

After resting with him for a while, we journeyed further up the mountain and came upon an ashram in the middle of nowhere. Except for the guru and the young boys who cooked for him, we were all alone. This was the ashram of Mauna Babaji, known as the silent guru. At seven years old, he had wandered out the door from his privileged home in Delhi, called to the Himalayas. After many years of wandering, he had found his way to this spot, and had spent twelve years in silence, meditating naked in the snow. He had ended his years of silence just a few years before we arrived.

Wearing long, red, velveteen robes, and dreadlocks down to his ankles, he greeted us, saying that he had had a vision the night before that two people would be coming to visit him, and that he had a meal prepared and waiting for us. Sure enough, the meal was hot and waiting. After eating, he ushered us into the inner sanctum of his temple, a small room adorned with red velvet walls, heavily laden altars with candles and burning incense.

Pritam and the guru began an animated conversation in Hindi that I did not understand. Mauna Babaji had a beatific presence. As they talked, he laughed frequently, and every time he laughed, I felt bathed in joy and bliss. As they continued talking, I closed my eyes to meditate. At some point, the two of them fell silent, and it felt as though the three of us had descended together into a deep meditative state. I was filled with a profound sense of bliss and happiness.

While in this state, I heard a voice in my head say, "You were Mauna Babaji's mother." At that moment, I opened my eyes to find Mauna Babaji looking deeply into my eyes. Without a word from me about what I had just heard in my meditation, the guru took my hands in his and said, "Yes, it is true. You were my mother." And then he got up off his seat, put a garland of leaves around my head, and bowed at my feet. I was rendered completely speechless. I mean, really! How does the mind grok such a moment? I don't know how to explain it, or what it actually means, other than to say, it happened.

One day, after returning from the Chardham Yatra trip, I was sitting in my counseling office reflecting on Mauna Babaji. It occurred to me that, had I been born in India instead of the States, I would have likely ended up like him. He wasn't all that different from me. He sits, in his ashram, and receives whoever shows up, and offers his love and wisdom. I sit in my office in Mill Valley, California, receive whoever shows up, and offer my love and wisdom as well. Here in the West, the only path to that kind of service is psychology, psychotherapy, coaching, or counseling. No clear path exists here for being a spiritual guide or healer; those of us called to such service often become therapists or life coaches. Years later, when I sat with the world-renowned Western spiritual teacher Ram Dass, he confided to me that had he not found his way to India and met his guru back in the early '60s, he likely would have ended up where I was; in an office in Mill Valley, as a therapist. I told him that had I found my way to India earlier and met my guru, I'd have likely ended up where he was . . .

Part 4
Surrender

Crack me open . . .
Let every mistaken and false notion
spill out of me and onto the earth.
Empty me
Until I can no longer claim, "I know."
Let me gather in my hands that which has spilled,
And with the tenderest of love,
offer it to the wind.
And may I stand naked and new,
Knowing absolutely nothing
And absolutely everything.

CHAPTER 9

Moment of Truth

THE DAY AFTER I received those fateful anonymous letters from England, Pritam finally called to "explain" his betrayal. After three and a half years in relationship with him, I prepared for the worst.

"Hi . . .." Pritam sounds distant, hesitant, and sheepish.

"Hi," I say back. More excruciating silence. He mutters something in a tortured voice. I have stopped breathing.

"What happened?" More silence. "WHAT THE FUCK HAPPENED?!" I shout down the phone. Utterly confused, I'm still hoping beyond reason he has some explanation. I desperately want to believe he's not been having an affair and that I have not been betrayed.

"I want to tell you everything but I don't want to tell you on the phone. Can't I tell you tomorrow when you pick me up at the airport? I will tell you everything in person."

"WHAT THE FUCK HAPPENED?! I DON'T WANT TO SEE YOU IN PERSON UNTIL YOU TELL ME WHAT HAPPENED. TELL ME *NOW*!"

I am screaming, coming unglued, out of control, desperate, head exploding, heart breaking. Before I slam down the phone, I hear him say,

"She was a Reiki healer who came to the house to do some energy work on me. She seduced me . . . put my cock in her mouth . . ."

That was more than I wanted or needed to hear. I hung up, and started shaking violently—screaming, crying, yelling, rocking my body as if to soothe a crying infant. How could this be happening? How could this be real? *What the fuck is going on?!* My whole world was spinning out of control, my heart and mind splintering; nothing made sense, and all I could do was rock myself and wail a primordial sound that rose up from the depths of my being and wracked me until I was exhausted.

He texted back, pleading to be able to tell me the whole story in person. I responded,

"I will not be coming to pick you up at the airport. Instead, you will take the airporter to the bus station, get a cab to my house, pick up your car, and then find some other place to stay for the five days you are in town."

"Please, please, please hear me out," he said. "I promise I will tell you everything. I just don't want to tell you over the phone. *Please.*"

"Okay," I said steely, "I will hear you out but you need to find someplace else to stay."

"You can't really mean that," he said incredulously. "You won't let me stay there?"

That was too much. I screamed back in text: "YOU WILL TAKE THE AIRPORTER TO THE BUS STATION. TAKE A *FUCKING* CAB TO THE HOUSE, AND I WILL

HEAR YOU OUT. THEN YOU WILL FIND SOME
OTHER *FUCKING* PLACE TO STAY. *YOU FUCKING
ASSHOLE!*"

He arrived at my home the next evening at 10:30.

"I'm thirsty, may I have some water?" he announced as he
walked in—apparently expecting me to lovingly bring him a
glass of honeyed water, as I would usually do for him after a
long trip from overseas.

"The glasses and water are in the kitchen. Get your own
drink if you're thirsty."

We sat on the couch in the living room and I waited for
him to begin. He didn't. Instead, just another thunderous
silence. By this time, I was sure his admission over the phone
was merely the tip of a yet-to-be-revealed iceberg. His excuse
that the woman had seduced him didn't ring true, of course;
besides, if it had happened once, I was sure it wasn't an isolat-
ed incident. Sitting there in front of him, the sting of betrayal
opening my eyes to a reality I didn't want to face, I was certain his "confession" would be, at best a bunch of half truths
or, more likely, a tangle of lies.

And then I had a moment of inspiration:

"It's 10:30 and I'm exhausted. If you don't start talking in
the next five minutes, you will need to leave. Assume I have
already spoken with the person involved, and that I already
know *everything*. What interests me now is seeing how honest
you are actually willing to be."

It was a total bluff. I had no idea yet who the other woman
was: She had gone to great lengths to conceal her identity by

typing the letters so her handwriting could not be recognized, and had not provided a forwarding address. Nevertheless, under duress and probably still jet-lagged, Pritam believed me and, torturously, started spilling out the entire sordid, shocking, inconceivable story.

He had met her more than a year and a half earlier, just after our pilgrimage to the Himalayas. On that trip, we had navigated dangerously steep and twisted mountain paths, traveled roads washed out by monsoon-like rains, surrounded always by breathtakingly beautiful snow-covered peaks; our days peppered with transcendent experiences at temples and shrines, visits with holy men and rituals with temple Brahmins—this "journey of a lifetime" had touched our souls. Back at Rishikesh, we had stood together in the waters of the Ganges, exchanged rings and shared vows of love and commitment.

We had flown on separate planes from Delhi and reunited in the airport at Singapore for an hour before his flight back to England to resume his summer teaching. I had returned to the States.

According to his story, he had met her at a 5Rhythms ecstatic dance in England and she had seduced him on the dance floor. He later learned she was a linguistics student as well as a Reiki healer. He imagined he could use her for some linguistics work, and that she could do some healing on a friend of his who was dying. They met at his friend's house for a Reiki session, and afterwards, because it was late, she didn't want to take the bus all the way back to London, so he offered to let her stay in the downstairs bedroom of his country house. Apparently, she had crept upstairs during the night as he slept, and seduced him. As if that alone wasn't unbelievable, he went on to tell me she was also an experienced Tantra practitioner and that he "wanted to learn some new techniques" from her to bring home to me. Getting this much of the story out of him felt like forcing a cat to cough up a hairball. I asked for her name.

"Tania," he spluttered indignantly.

"Tania what?" I demanded.

"I don't think I need to tell you that," he replied defiantly.

"Then this conversation is over," I declared, and ushered him out the door, unwittingly slamming it on his elbow as he left.

I sat back down on the couch, destroyed. A year-and-a-half? He had been carrying on this affair all that time? I replayed the last eighteen months of my life, and realized his affair was already underway when I had flown to meet him in India that December with my two children and best friend. Throughout the time he had been living with me—from January through July, including our "moonhoney" trip to Costa Rica—he had betrayed me. Every day since Costa Rica, and every email, text message, and phone call, where he professed his love for me, pouring out his longing and desire, he had been carrying on this affair with her. *How could that happen?* It all seemed utterly inconceivable. Yet, here it was: My entire life, everything I thought I knew about reality, was unraveling. Everything I had felt, everything I had experienced, everything I had believed was now completely shattered, in ruins at my feet.

I texted him:

"Since you are in town for five days before flying back to Cambridge, you have two hours tomorrow during these specific times . . . and three hours the following day, during these specific times . . . to get all of your shit boxed up and out of my house."

He arrived the next day at the appointed hour and, in strained silence, I watched him begin packing up his things from what had been "our" home. He returned the following day with a couple of guys to help, finished boxing up all of his stuff, and in the pouring rain loaded it into his van. I had no idea where he was staying and I didn't care. I stood there, in each room, as he packed up his belongings, wanting him to feel the destruction and devastation he had caused to our home and our life together. He looked like a broken man as we now both reeled through the aftermath of his tsunami of deceit . . . nothing but broken shards of painful emotions in a home once filled with laughter and love, futures and dreams.

Before he left, he asked if we could talk, pleading, "Can't you forgive me? Can't we work this out? Hilary forgave Bill, why can't you forgive me? I promise it will never happen again. It was a mistake. I love you."

Everything in me wanted to believe those promises. Everything in me wanted to go back to the way things were. *Everything.* I looked at him and simply said, "I don't know."

The following day, he boarded the plane and was on his way to Cambridge. For the next several months of email and text dialogues, he bounced back and forth between begging forgiveness and alternately blaming everyone and everything but himself for what had happened. He referred to the "other woman," and all the other women in his life who had ever loved him, as piranhas out to devour his soul. He got defensive, and minimized what he had done. At times, he also turned combative and hostile. He did everything, except open up, become vulnerable, accountable, and able to understand what had led him to have the affair in the first place.

In the meantime, I did some investigative work of my own. I needed to know who this woman was and to get the entire story, or at least her version. I remembered "Tania" was part of a group email he had sent out several months earlier announcing the death of a beloved colleague. Not being the jealous type, I hadn't thought much of this—evidence of my ability to not see what was right in front of me.

I went through my emails, found her address, and, assuming she was the "Tania" in question, contacted her. I thanked her for sending me the letters and helping to open my eyes.

"Apparently we have both loved and been deceived by the same man. Perhaps you can understand my need and desire to talk with you and ask some questions. Would you be willing to talk with me?" She agreed, for which I will always be grateful. We arranged a time to connect on Skype, though neither of us opted for video. Needless to say, her version of the story was quite different from his.

They *had* met at a 5Rhythms ecstatic dance a year and a half before. *He* had seduced *her* on the dance floor, and then pursued her. He had told her about a woman out in California, but that the relationship was over, leading her to believe he was available for a relationship. She had fallen in love with him. Apparently, after eighteen months, as he prepared to leave for the States, he had planned on ending it with her to return to me. When she discovered that he and I were very much still together—in fact, had talked about getting married and buying a home—she, understandably, flew into a rage. That's when things turned ugly between them. According to Tania, Pritam was so emotionally abusive she blocked his emails, and when she realized he was living a double life with me in California, she assumed I probably didn't know anything about his "other" life in England, either. Whether motivated by revenge or wanting to stop this man from hurting another woman any further, she made it her business to let me know what had been happening on the other side of the world. She also let me know that, serendipitously, she had found out he had had another affair during our time together. I remain grateful to Tania regardless of her motivations. She helped me wake up to my own denial—fortunately before I had committed my life and had entangled my finances with this man.

During the many months of conversation that followed while he taught at Cambridge, he finally did confess everything—including his affair with the other woman before Tania. He had been married for twenty years before I met him, and his wife had died of cancer. As she lay dying, he had an affair; in fact, had many affairs throughout their marriage. Later, I discovered he never had a faithful relationship with any woman. Clearly, Pritam was a career philanderer, and I just happened to be last in a long line of women who had loved him, and whom he had betrayed. I was, however, the first one with whom he got caught.

Only years later, after I had learned of his affairs and my world fell apart, did I realize I was dealing with a full-blown, textbook case of diagnosable Narcissistic Personality Disorder. The *Diagnostic And Statistical Manual For Mental Disorders*, 4th Edition (DSM IV), the bible of psychological diagnoses from the American Psychiatric Association, lists the following criteria:

1. An exaggerated sense of self-importance. *Check!*
2. Preoccupation with fantasies of unlimited success, power, brilliance, beauty, or ideal love. *Check!*
3. Believes he is "special" and can only be understood by, or should associate with, other special or high-status people (or institutions). *Check!*
4. Requires excessive admiration. *Check!*
5. Has a sense of entitlement. *Check!*
6. Selfishly takes advantage of others to achieve his own ends. *Check!*
7. Lacks empathy. *Check!*

8. Is often envious of others or believes that others are envious of him. *Check!*

9. Shows arrogant, haughty, patronizing, or contemptuous behaviors or attitudes. *Check! Check! Check!*

Following that initial trip to India, he continued to accuse me of infidelities throughout the rest of our relationship. He even hacked into my computer, read my personal emails, copied and saved them, and then when he had built what he thought was a fool-proof case of my guilt, he threw them at me. Instead of throwing him out then and there, I lovingly reassured him that when he realized how foolish he was, he would be mortified. I went through each email and explained what they were and weren't about, and for months continued to do my best to reassure him. Even though he repeatedly promised he had stopped hacking into my computer, he continued to do so, denying and lying about it every time I inquired.

He also tracked the GPS on my car looking for proof of my alleged dalliances. He installed a caller ID on our home-office phone to track my calls. I didn't learn about all of this until much later, and so did not respond as I should have to his aggressive, hostile, and emotionally abusive accusations and suspicions. When I collapsed in tears out of sheer hurt and frustration, he showed a complete lack of empathy. Instead, he used his brilliant mind to twist the conversation so thoroughly that I often ended up more confused, lost, and bewildered.

Pritam's sense of entitlement frequently manifested as an expectation that *I should know what he wanted without his having to ask,* and then he would get hostile, angry, and belittling when he didn't get it. If I spent time with other friends or family he immediately felt abandoned, and would punish me with more emotional abuse and character assassination. Almost everyone in my close circle of family and friends found him arrogant, pedantic, inflated, and self-absorbed, and tolerated him because I loved him. I ignored the warning signs.

Like any classic narcissistic personality, he had legions of admirers the world over—professional colleagues and acquaintances he had charmed with his charisma and brilliant mind. Typically, the person most intimately involved with a narcissist bears the brunt of their rage and feels the consequences of their sense of entitlement. Narcissists masterfully present themselves to the world as exceptionally congenial, generous, and altruistic. In fact, being universally admired by colleagues and casual friends, narcissists can easily convince their partners that *they* must be the crazy ones. Countless times, after one of his raging outbursts that demolished me emotionally, we would leave the house and then I'd watch him hold court with colleagues and friends, charming and regaling them with stories of his brilliance—*as if nothing had happened between us.*

Pritam, a world-renowned scholar, taught at many of the world's most prestigious universities. Highly respected in academia, only the women who have loved him the most know his secrets.

The key question, of course, is not why did he treat me that way—but *why did I stay?* After all, I do have an advanced degree in psychology, have counseled thousands of couples, and taught couples retreats and workshops for more than twenty-five years. Given that background, you might well think I would (or *should)* have seen him for what he was, and gotten the fuck out of Dodge. But I didn't. Why?

Beginning with that first trip to India, just six months into our relationship, some part of me knew something was very wrong. But I loved this man, deeply. A nagging voice in the back of my mind knew all through the three-and-a-half years of our relationship that it was unhealthy, emotionally destructive and damaging, yet I doggedly stayed on. Why? I considered myself a self-respecting, conscious, awake woman; not someone who would choose to stay in an abusive relationship—and yet I chose to stay.

CHAPTER 10

Shattered Innocence

LEARNING ABOUT PRITAM's affairs had hit me like a slap in the face—a wake-up call to get brutally honest with myself. Three-plus years of emotional abuse had choked the life out of our relationship; his affairs were just the final blow. Even then, I remained open to reconciliation for months afterwards, until it became undeniably obvious that this man was incapable of ever behaving differently. He had lived sixty years of lies and deceit, all the way back to his impoverished childhood in Fiji. Healing those wounds would take years of committed intensive therapy. He needed to understand and embrace the demons tormenting his soul—and that would work *only if* he could truly acknowledge he had a problem. I could no longer be collateral damage for his healing journey.

I reflected on our years together—remembering the many times he had been emotionally cruel to me, hostile, suspicious, accusatory, demeaning, belittling, dismissive, lying, and deceiving. Every time he had treated me that way, I had tried harder and harder to bring him more love, more kindness, more forgiveness, more understanding, more compassion, more empathy, more patience. Many, if not most, women would have told him to "fuck off" after that first trip to India together—and certainly after discovering he had repeatedly hacked into their computer. Not me. *Why?*

I had to ask myself, "Where did I learn this behavior? When and where had I learned to love someone no matter how he treated me? When had I learned to distort reality to the degree that when someone dismissed me or treated me cruelly, I could convince myself it was a form of kindness and love? Where, when, and with whom did I learn that's how I could get love—that I should love more, love harder, forgive more, no matter how I was being treated?"

As any psychologist or Psychology 101 book would tell you, I didn't have to look further than my own childhood and, in particular, my relationship with my father. Just like my Indian lover Pritam, my father was a charismatic and intelligent man, alternately loving and emotionally cruel. He, too, was notoriously narcissistic, so much so, in fact, our family often joked about how he called himself "America's Guest." He felt entitled the world should provide him whatever he wanted; and, because of his superior intellect and humor, he expected I'd be his loyal and adoring audience.

When my mother abandoned me, my father was all I had. As a two-and-a-half-year-old, I clung to him, a life raft in a turbulent, scary ocean, and I learned very quickly that the best way to ensure his love and protection was to be his adoring daughter. I laughed at his jokes, gave him physical affection, and became dumb, deaf, and blind to his frequent hurtful and demeaning comments about my body, my boyfriends, my feelings, my beliefs, my attitudes, and, later, even my choice of profession. Despite his physical affection, our shared sense of humor, and knowing he did genuinely love and cherish me, his biting remarks cut me down at the knees, leaving my sense of self-worth and self-esteem in tatters. Very early on, I developed a fierce resistance to admitting to myself the truth about his downside. I desperately *needed* to believe in him as an all-good, all-loving father. I desperately *needed* to find a way to ignore, deny, repress, or disappear any evidence that threatened my positive perception of him. In order to preserve the illusion, I *had* to engage in self-betrayal and to deny my own authentic experience whenever he treated me harshly. To see him as "Good Daddy," I had to believe his criticisms and belittlements of me. As a result, I began to actively engage in my own self-betrayal, self-abandonment, and self-criticism at a very early age. Of course, being so young, I wasn't consciously aware of making any of these decisions; it was simply what I *had* to do to preserve a desperately needed illusion of my all-loving father.

If I hadn't constructed an illusion I could feel safe in, the alternative would have killed me. To have consciously acknowledged that my father was as capable of harming me emotionally as he was of loving me and keeping me safe would have shattered my fragile world, plunging me into terror and isolation. As a young child, I could not allow myself to feel that. As children, we are utterly and completely dependent on our parents (or some other primary caregiver) for our literal survival. As instinctual animals, we do what we have to do in order to survive. After the loss of my mother, I could not afford to feel emotionally abandoned by my father as well. The fact that I managed to suppress consciously feeling that debilitating aloneness and terror does not mean I *wasn't* feeling it; I had merely pushed the pain down into my unconscious.

However, the strategy of loving someone "no matter what"—turning a blind eye to abuse or abandonment, fiercely creating and preserving an illusion I could believe in despite so much evidence to the contrary—became my "default" in all my relationships from then on. This strategy remained unconscious because the degree of self-betrayal and self-abandonment I had to engage in *prevented* me from even knowing I was distorting reality. The problem with being asleep is you're asleep! I believed in people's goodness no matter how cruel they might be to me. I adopted the persona of the kind, compassionate, endlessly forgiving, and understanding friend. I was often the last one hanging onto friendships with people that others had long ago given up on because they were unkind, selfish, self-absorbed. I prided myself on "hanging in there" in relationships; developed sophisticated belief systems about the value of "working on your relationships," worked harder, tried harder, hung in there longer than just about anybody else I know—all the while believing I was merely giving people the benefit of the doubt, intent on demonstrating the power of love, compassion, and empathy. After all, isn't that what we learn from spiritual teachers and wisdom keepers?

While all of that is true—and despite everything that has happened, I still hold those values near and dear—in my case, I also wanted to protect myself from seeing people for who they truly were. I tried hard to preserve my relationships, whatever the costs to me.

Eventually, I woke up the hard way: by confronting my lover's betrayal and, going deeper, by also confronting my patterns of self-betrayal. I had to face how much I had distorted reality in my drive to preserve love at any cost—*and why*. Forced to see the whole truth about my father, and how I had denied and suppressed his emotional abuse, I finally woke up from a fifty-year slumber. It all came crashing into my awareness, and I began to grieve the anguish the little girl in me had known on some level all along, but could not afford to feel at the time.

Decades of accumulated grief exploded from deep within me, like a volcanic eruption. Not only did I grieve the end of my relationship with Pritam, and the years of his deceptions and betrayals, I also had to release a lifetime of pent-up pain as I faced the truth about my father, along with the even more sobering anguish over my own self-betrayal and abandonment. I experienced a tsunami of grief that left me nearly incapable of functioning. Somehow, I managed to get up every morning and get my daughter fed and off to school. Somehow, I managed to go to work every day and put this internal holocaust out of my mind just long enough to be present for my clients' lives and their struggles. I even managed, somehow, to take a group of women to Costa Rica on a previously scheduled women's retreat, and I also managed to begin teaching a year-long previously scheduled couples group. But inside, I felt like the walking dead. And if I wasn't already dead, most of me wanted to be. When I didn't have to be "on," I would often hunker down in the womb-like safety and comfort of my bed, releasing what felt like a bottomless ocean of tears and grief. I felt like a raw nerve, too raw to be exposed in public, and withdrew from most of my usual social engagements. On one occasion, after crying so hard and for so long, I scared myself and called one of my closest women friends; she came over and held me through the night, allowing me to feel where I began and ended.

Everything I had ever believed in—about myself, about love, about relationships, about who I'm supposed to be, and about what love is supposed to provide—fractured and came crashing down. I had no solid ground beneath me anymore, nothing I felt sure of, nothing I believed in, nothing and no one I could trust, least of all myself. I could no longer sustain whatever pride my ego had taken in being a "love guru" or expert relationship coach. Humbled and brought to my knees, I had no choice but to surrender everything I thought I knew or was. Before this, nothing in my life had pushed me into such deep and transformative surrender.

And then . . . if that was not enough, my father suddenly and unexpectedly died!

Just four months after learning of Pritam's betrayals, already drowning in despair and grief, I flew down to L.A. to say goodbye to my father's dead body.

He had been admitted to the hospital a few days earlier, disoriented as if he'd had a stroke. The ER staff determined he had not stroked, but that his kidneys were blocked by an enlarged prostrate, and, most likely, he had not urinated for a few days—leaving his body full of toxins. After an emergency procedure to the artery in his neck, they flushed out the toxins. At 9:30 AM the day he died, I was on the phone with my brother who had just spoken with the doctor, who told him that all my father's vital signs were normal and stabilized. He was eating and drinking normally, was cognitively coherent, and would likely be released in the next few days.

As it happened, while on the phone with my brother, I had just arrived to meet Pritam for breakfast near my home in Marin—part of our ongoing dialogues to see if we could work things out. I got off the phone with Kenny, sat down in the restaurant (the same one, as it turned out, where we had lingered over breakfast and then lunch, followed by our first kiss), and told Pritam about my father.

"Well, I'll be down in L.A. in a few weeks, maybe I could look in on him?" he offered.

"Did it not occur to you," I said, "that perhaps my father would not want to see you—the man who just betrayed his daughter and broke her heart?"

He seemed oblivious to the possibility that the people in my life who love me and care about me might have feelings about his affairs as well. His sense of entitlement extended to believing he should be able to behave however he wanted, no matter how abhorrent, and that there should be no consequences. Typical of a narcissist, he got hostile and enraged whenever confronted with the negative impact of his behaviors. He became belligerent, angry, and combative . . . Needless to say, the breakfast did not go well. Rather than going for a walk as planned, we decided to go see a movie. Sitting in that darkened movie theater with the man who had broken my heart—watching, of all things, *My Week With Marilyn*, a movie based on the true story of Marilyn Monroe's affair with a young man while she was married to Joe DiMaggio—my father slipped away. He had fallen asleep in the hospital bed after eating lunch, and never woke up.

I didn't get the news until after Pritam and I had said our strained goodbyes. In the car on my way to pick up my daughter from her volleyball game, my cell phone rang:

"Tina, he's gone," my brother quietly said to me.

"Oh, my God! *No-o-o-o-o!*" I cried into the phone.

As I had done when my stepmother died unexpectedly, and again when I first learned about Pritam's affairs, I began rocking my body, instinctively trying to soothe the desperate and shattered little girl inside me.

"No, no, no, *no-o-o-o-o-o!* Not now, please! *I just can't take any more loss!* Why now?!*"

I called my ex-husband to come help me figure out what to do. Waiting for Maya after her volleyball game, I walked in circles around the parking lot, sobbing, trying to comprehend how, yet again, my world could fall apart even more. *How could my father be dead?* I have never existed in this world without him—the only person who has been with me my entire life. How could I possibly continue without him? Once again, I found myself falling off a cliff I didn't even know I was standing on.

My ex-husband, God bless him, rushed to meet me, grabbed me in his arms, held me while we both cried (he had been very close to my father), followed me back to my house, prepared dinner for our daughter, helped me make arrangements to fly down to L.A. the next day, and took Maya home with him so I could collapse into my blinding grief.

I managed somehow to call all of the clients I was scheduled to see the next day, and then boarded a plane the next morning for LAX. My brother Kenny met me at the airport and, together with his wife and daughter, we headed straight for my father's room at the assisted living facility where he had been living. We went through his belongings and packed them up. My mind buzzed with memories: Here was a man who had been a vaudevillian comedian, an acrobat, a drummer in a jazz trio, the star quarterback at Brooklyn College, an avid historian, salesman, lover of life, lover of women, playboy, father, brother, son. Now, all his 86 years of living had been reduced to a few boxes of belongings in this little room where he had spent the last five years. Most of what we packed and boxed turned out to be photos and memorabilia from his show-business career, along with hundreds of newspaper clippings from his glory days as a quarterback. How does an entire life get reduced to a few boxes of treasured memories, bags of trash, and clothes for Goodwill?

By mid-day we were done, and it was time to go view my father's body. Kenny chose not to see him, preferring to remember my father as he had seen him in the hospital the day before he died. I had last seen him four months before, when I had gone to L.A. to visit him for his 86th birthday, just a week before learning about Pritam's affairs. Our visit had been a bit strained due to significant signs of dementia; and, without any self-censorship, he went on and on about the "ugly" women who lived at the assisted living facility. His unconstrained and obnoxious comments about the women there offended me, and I told him so. I asked him to stop, but he belligerently refused. Disgusted, I excused myself and walked away. However, perhaps because of the early unexpected loss of my mother, I have always made a practice of telling people I love them before I say goodbye, whether in person or on the phone, just in case I never see them again. Thankfully, the last words my father heard from me when I stopped by for a brief visit the next day on my way to the airport, were "I love you."

Because Kenny elected not to see my father, I had the opportunity to be alone with him. Shaking, crying, and unsure of what it would be like to see his dead body, I went in. I had prepared myself for this moment my entire life—because I had lost my mother at such a young age, I always waited for the other shoe to drop, painfully aware that loved ones can disappear without warning. I pulled up a chair to sit next to the cardboard coffin. What I experienced next surprised me: As I looked at my father's corpse, the small room filled with an unexpected grace. Through a small window, I noticed the day had turned cloudy and overcast. This man, who had been such a significant and important influence in my life, with whom I had such a complex web of feelings and attachments, looked small inside the coffin, as if the enormity of the "Father" archetype he had expressed throughout my life had dissolved, and he had now returned to the human scale of just a man.

I placed my right hand at his heart and my left hand at the crown of his head, and as I rubbed his heart, I experienced deep gratitude for everything—the good, the bad, and the ugly. From a place of undeniable knowing, I *knew* he had loved and cherished me as deeply as was possible for him; and I also knew that *he knew I had loved him*, too. I could now see the beauty of everything I had become *because* of the father he had been, and *because* of all of the things I had had to struggle with inside myself for having had him as my father. Beyond our personalities, I could feel the sacred contract between us. I forgave him for everything he didn't know how to do better, and asked for his forgiveness as well. I knew we had come together in this life to teach each other exactly the lessons we each had needed, and that our work together was complete. I thanked him out loud:

"I know you loved me, and I know you know how much I loved you. Our work together is done. Thank you. I love you."

At that exact moment, the sun burst through the clouds, and a beam of sunlight shot through the tiny window, miraculously falling right on my father and I—as if bathing both of us in unconditional love, peace, understanding, and well-being. I tucked a piece of his football memorabilia inside his folded hands, kissed his forehead, unwrapped and held his feet in the palms of my hands, and exited the room in a profound state of peace.

As I walked down the hallway to meet Kenny, happy memories from my childhood came flooding back: the times my father would let me ride on his shoulders; the times he would make us both laugh until we cried; the times he held me in his arms and let me fall asleep in his lap. . . . After months feeling deep anguish over his emotional cruelties, I felt I had finally reached a place of balance. Now at fifty, I could hold in my heart, with compassion and understanding, the whole truth about my father—including his cruelties and kindnesses. I no longer needed to deny, repress, or pretend anything. I now had the grace to see it all as it was, to understand the perfection of it all, and to finally find a resting place inside my heart.

At least, that was how I, as a fifty-year old woman, dealt with his death. The young girl inside me, however, started spiraling into a terrifying abyss. Could I exist without him? Was I now completely alone and orphaned in this big scary world? To her, going on without him seemed impossible, and many months of grieving, crying, and loss followed. Sometimes, the pain grew so unbearable it threatened to splinter my weary psyche into a million shards. For months, I would cry unexpectedly at seemingly insignificant and unrelated events. For months, I just had to surrender again, and again, and again, to the waves of loss and grief washing over and through me. At some point, I no longer even knew anymore what exactly I grieved. My sadness no longer felt specific to the loss of Pritam, or his betrayals, or to my own betrayals, or to the loss of my father. Looking back, I see how the remnants of fifty years of unfelt and unexpressed grief had to purge themselves from the recesses of my psyche and the cells of my body. I squeezed out every last drop of grief, and, in time, I could do nothing more than simply surrender and say to myself:

"Yes, I will feel this. Yes, I will meet this. Yes, I will endure this. Yes, I will surrender to this. Yes, I will allow this to strip me bare. . . . Yes, yes, yes. I surrender."

He who learns must suffer,
and, even in our sleep,
pain that cannot forget
falls drop by drop upon the heart,
and in our own despair, against our will,
comes wisdom to us by the awful grace of God.

— Aeschylus

CHAPTER 11

———— ❧ ————

Why Have You Forsaken Me?

RIGHT AT A point when I believed I had absolutely nothing left to give, the "gods" demanded yet more sacrifice from me. I didn't realize it at the time, but I still had to contend with another layer of dismantling and deconstruction.

For most of my life, I aimed for intimacy and relationship as my Holy Grail. I had always believed relationship to be a spiritual path, and my husband Keith and I had consciously used our marriage for mutual learning, growing, and healing. I taught couples' workshops and retreats for years, guiding partners how to mine the riches of their relationship, how to seek for and find the Beloved in themselves and their partner, how to bring loving kindness and forgiveness to moments of discord. I had always, unwittingly, tethered my relationship with God to my relationship with an outer "Other."

Following the breakup with Pritam and now with my father gone, I found myself unexpectedly bereft not only of the outer relationships that had sustained me, but also of my connection to God. Relationship had been my "oxygen," or, perhaps more accurately, my "drug of choice." I had never been addicted to substances as a way to transcendence; but love, intimacy, and sexuality were my paths to God. Now, suddenly without them, I was like a heroin addict without a fix.

I became desperate, trolling on-line dating sites, looking for my "Mr. Right." Very few profiles sparked any interest in me, and those that did were either not interested in a woman with a young child still at home or I was not interested in them. I had always been a woman who could attract a man. I had *never* not been able to find a lover if I wanted one. Suddenly, I was fifty-years old, middle-aged, and had lost my mojo. The harder it became to find a date, the more insanely desperate I became, responding to any and all on-line profiles whether or not I was really interested. I *needed* a date like an addict needs a fix.

The first "fish" I caught left after five minutes when he discovered I still had a child living with me. I spent my second date with a man who talked the entire evening about another woman he was still in love with. As he took my credit card to help pay for dinner, he informed me he had always paid for her when they went out together. I sobbed in my car all the way home. I wasn't even interested in him, just miserable, lonely, feeling ugly, over-the-hill, unwanted, invisible. I wanted a fix—someone to make me feel attractive, desirable; someone who could be my portal to God. "Please, just shoot me up *now*. I DESPERATELY NEED A FIX!"

I met a guy on-line and we ended up having sex—the first time since my "moonhoney" in Costa Rica. More than a year since anyone had touched my body, I needed it like a fish out of water gasps for air. He turned out to be a great lover—playful, creative, generous, easy, and I gulped down that "air" like my life depended on it. However, while my body had received something it desperately needed, afterwards I knew that was not what I really wanted. Disconnected from my heart—from my soul, from my mind, from my entire self—sex was simply just that: fun and enjoyable, but not transcendent. It lacked the spiritual connection I longed for with a true Beloved.

A vague whispering grew louder in my head, calling me back to the ritual I had facilitated in Costa Rica for my fiftieth birthday . . . "A Woman Unto Myself. A Woman Unto Myself." If I had had any idea of the sacrifices that would be asked of me to live into that prayer, I would have thought long and hard about it! Thankfully, ignorance is bliss, and life had its way with me before I could really protest. Rising up from somewhere deep within me, I began to feel a pull away from needing or wanting an outer relationship with a man. Everything in me resisted the unconscious wisdom of my psyche. *I wanted my drug.* And I wanted it *now*! I wanted only *my* drug—nothing else would do. Like a belligerent-yet-exhausted teenager refusing to go to bed, I resisted with all my might, even though I knew that's what I needed to do. Stubbornly, I kept trolling dating sites, went out on meaningless dates, and steadfastly refused to heed the call from my soul to turn inwards. Instead, I ranted at the universe: "I WANT A RELATIONSHIP. GIVE ME A MAN, DAMN IT! GIVE HIM TO ME NOWWWWW!" Absolutely nothing I did worked. Apparently, the universe had conspired to prevent me from shooting up, and I did not handle the withdrawal gracefully.

For "rehab," I went away on a weekend retreat to Monterey with two of my best girlfriends—two women I love and cherish, both of whom have deep and abiding spiritual paths. One is married, the other has been divorced for many years, has a deep and life-sustaining relationship with God, and really couldn't care less whether or not she ever has another relationship with a man. I could never understand that about her. I secretly believed she was in denial, or afraid, or too wounded to ever let another man into her heart. Her marriage and divorce had been brutal. As I listened to her talk that weekend, something else began to make itself known to me. She really was *completely fine* without a man in her life; she was happy and fulfilled, deeply connected to her God and her faith, open to the possibility of a wonderful man showing up in her life, but not *needing* one to feel whole and complete. Rather than secretly questioning her, I began to envy her. She had something I desperately wanted.

The three of us went for a long walk on the beach, and when I began to feel tired I sat down on a driftwood log to meditate, letting my two friends walk on. After awhile, I felt the need to lie on the earth, so I laid myself down, resting my head against the log, and began playing with the sand. Suddenly, and unexpectedly, I started to heave with loud sobs that seemed to emanate from the core of my being. I didn't know exactly why; I just felt desperately *alone*. I lost track of time, and when I sat up and looked around, my friends had vanished. I felt utterly abandoned on the deserted beach. I sobbed my guts up, but no one knew, and no one cared. "I could die right here, sitting on this log, all alone, completely forsaken, wracked by grief, and no one would notice." I allowed myself to go all the way into the experience. Like Christ on the cross, I laid my head slanted on the log, put my arms out as if holding the cross, and cried out to the universe, "Why Hast Thou Forsaken Me?" I sobbed, and sobbed, and sobbed until nothing was left of me. Only then did I hear the faintest whisper speak back to me:

"Don't you understand, I have not forsaken you? I'm just trying to direct you away from the well where you have always gone to drink. That well can no longer nourish you. It is too small a source for what you seek. I have not forsaken you; I am trying to point you toward the true source that will actually feed your soul, quench your thirst, and satiate your hunger. I am right here holding you." Then the reassuring voice drifted off into silence.

"Oh, well, why didn't you just say so!" I replied, as much to myself as to the mysterious Voice.

As once the winged energy of delight
carried you over childhood's dark abysses,
now beyond your own life build the great
arch of unimagined bridges.
Wonders happen if we can succeed
in passing through the harshest danger;
but only in a bright and purely granted
achievement can we realize the wonder.
To work with things in the indescribable
relationship is not too hard for us;
the pattern grows more intricate and subtle,
and being swept along is not enough.
Take your practiced powers and stretch them out
until they span the chasm between two
contradictions. . . . For the god
wants to know himself in you.

— Rilke

CHAPTER 12

A Woman Unto Herself

WHO AM I, then, if not a woman desperately needing a relationship? Won't I be lonely? Will I die alone? Who will hold me as I grow old, infirm, and frail? Don't I want the companionship of a friend, a lover? Don't I want someone to snuggle up to as I fall asleep at night? Don't I want someone making love to my body, someone to travel with, someone to make plans with, someone who asks how my day was?

What does it mean to be "a woman unto myself?" I have always loved men, beginning with my father. I have always enjoyed the juicy challenges of intimacy. I have always rejoiced in the playfulness of sexuality and the delicious exploration of two bodies joined together as one. Am I to live without those things now for the rest of my life? What, then, exactly does it mean to be "a woman unto myself?"

Despite stubborn resistance to the whisperings of my soul, I eventually began to notice that my habitual self-talk about wanting or needing to be in a relationship did not necessarily match how I actually *felt*. When I stepped outside my life-long habitual beliefs and checked in with myself in present time, I realized how often I was perfectly happy to come home after work to an empty house and sprawl diagonally across my king-size bed. Many mornings I would wake up perfectly satisfied with my own thoughts, my own rhythms. I began to value having time to myself to focus on my own reveries—time that otherwise would have been occupied with the daily maintenance of a relationship.

Of course, sometimes I felt lonely; sometimes my body hungered for the touch of a man; sometimes I yearned for the simplicity of companionship, someone to go see a movie with; someone to hold my hand as we walked along the beach; someone to share plans for our future together. But just as often, I didn't miss any of that. I began to feel fine in my own company—even better, I began to feel exquisite bliss, joy, happiness, and contentment just being with *me*.

And here today I sit, back at the same house I rented at the beach last year to celebrate my 50th birthday. Tomorrow I celebrate turning fifty-one, exactly one year after I began writing this book. September 30 will mark a complete year from when I learned about my lover's affairs. January 29 will mark a full year since my father died. During the past twelve months, I have been completely turned inside out. Very little remains of the person I thought I was just one year ago. I have been, for the most part, completely dismantled and deconstructed. I have surrendered the relationship I once thought of as the greatest love of my life. I have surrendered most of the notions I had about myself, about love, about relationships, about life. I surrendered my father and sent his ashes out to sea.

A Woman Unto Herself

Now on the eve of my 51st birthday, I can feel how different I am from a year ago—the most emotionally brutal and wrenching year of my life. I have shed more tears in the past year than over the entire half century of my life. For a long, long time, I did not think I would survive this passage, certain I would fail, as Rilke says, to "practice my powers and stretch them out until they spanned the chasm between two contradictions . . ." certain I would never know the truth of his words: "For the god wants to know himself in you."

Today, I am not in a relationship, at least not with an outer Beloved. I find myself walking ever more assuredly toward the "God who wants to know himself within me." I sit here now, humbled by the massive renovations I have undergone. I know very little . . . and I wonder will I ever fall in love again in this lifetime? I don't know if I will feel lonely tomorrow or content in my aloneness. I look out at the Pacific Ocean and the soon-to-be-setting sun and feel gratitude for everything that has happened this past year. Strange as it might seem, I feel gratitude for my lover's betrayal; for the lightening-quick catalyst his deception provided for my spiritual deepening and emotional healing. I feel immense gratitude for my own resilient being that could weather the storms of these relentless tsunamis that lashed upon the shores of my life during the past twelve months, and that devastated everything I had clung to. I feel gratitude beyond expression for the friends who carried me aloft during my painful grieving process; who held me when I sobbed, who reminded me of my courage and strength when I felt I had none, who pointed me toward home when I lost my way, who listened endlessly to my pain and anguish, and who held the belief for me that I was falling together when all I could feel was falling apart. I do not know what the future holds for me, but I do know that right now, in this beautiful house on the beach, that has birthed this book, I am becoming, finally, a woman unto myself . . .

The sea foam laps around my bare feet
As seagulls scrounge through the remains of the day;
The watery sand mirrors streaks of setting sun
as it tucks itself in for the night behind the mountains.
I am left to reflect on a perfect day, and head for home.
A dark handsome man, visiting from Italy,
walks beside me a few paces.
Sharing the splendor of the sunset and the
seals playing alongside us in the surf.
He tells me I am beautiful, and then respectfully
allows me to move on,
Into my own solitude.

Epilogue

HERE I AM, back again at Stinson Beach—a year exactly to the day, from when I finished writing my story, two years from when I began writing it. I will remember the year 2012 as the most painful, wrenching, dismantling, deconstructing, renovating, transformational, and healing time of my life—at least, so far.

Early in February 2012, just five months after learning about Pritam's affairs, and just one month after my father's sudden and unexpected death, I was offered the opportunity to spend ten days with spiritual teacher and guru, Ram Dass, at his home on Maui, Hawaii. I arranged with Dassima, his devoted aide, to come to their home in December. I wanted to complete what felt like the most important year of my life in a very conscious and ritualistic way. Besides, I also had the rest of my father's ashes, which I wanted to return to Hawaii— the place he loved more than any other on the planet. He had lived there with my stepmom for years just before and after he retired. They had never been happier than when living in the islands, and Keith and I would visit them there every year when our son was young. My dad spent his days playing tennis and golf, and my mom spent her days sequestered in her painting studio, utterly and blissfully absorbed in her art. After her death, I discovered hundreds of her paintings, some of which still hang on the walls of my home to this day.

So, after an entire year spent mostly sobbing and grieving all of the losses, both inner and outer, I had endured that year, and after being completely dismantled down to the very bones of myself, and after having spent a year of being alone and beginning to find my way to becoming "a woman unto myself," in December of 2012, I boarded a plane bound for Maui. Dassima met me at the airport, took me to the local organic grocery store to pick up a few things I wanted to have at the house—and then, there I was, in Ram Dass' home, overlooking the Pacific Ocean, in beautiful sun-drenched Maui.

I was not to see my host until the next day, so after unpacking my bags and settling in, I went for a swim in the pool and then soaked in the hot tub. I laid my head back against the rim looking up into the tropical Maui sky, streaked with wispy pink-tinged clouds. Right above me, one had formed into a large rose-colored heart. Suddenly, my own heart flooded with love and burst wide open as it dawned on me that my "Year From Hell" ended here, in this very moment, soaking in Ram Dass' hot tub, surrounded by rose-colored, heart-shaped clouds! It seemed surreal. Overcome with a sense of grace and beauty, I experienced a profound knowing that my life was unfolding exactly as it was meant to, that everything that had happened in my life was exactly as it was meant to be, and that I had endured a year of what Ram Dass has called "Fierce Grace." Fierce grace, indeed!

I got up from the hot tub with a full, overflowing heart . . . grateful for my life exactly as it is, grateful that my year ended here, in this sacred place, in Ram Dass' home, with ten days ahead of me to spend with him, just him and me. As I stepped into the shower, a centipede greeted me by crawling up my leg! According to symbolic meaning, centipedes "alert us to new psychic environments and connections and to new and previously unrecognized psychic relationships." Well, all right then!

After showering, Ram Dass' personal chef Kelly cooked a delicious vegetarian meal. A loving and dedicated young woman, Kelly cooked all our meals while I was there. I slept peacefully like a baby that evening, and after breakfast the next morning, it was time to meet the man who inspired generations with his own style of westernized Eastern spiritual teaching.

Dassima showed me into the study, and there, sitting in his wheelchair, was Ram Dass. He beckoned me to a chair right in front of him, and as I approached, he stretched out his arms and announced, "You have such a radiant presence!" After a warm hug, he motioned for me to sit down and patted his wheelchair, inviting me to put my feet up beside him, which I did.

Instantly, I felt like we were old friends catching up. I told him about my "year from Hell," and he listened intently. In turn, he shared personal stories about his life, including "melodramas" he had endured—especially the stroke that had bound him to a wheelchair twelve years earlier. He talked about "fierce grace," and its power to destroy everything you thought you were, bringing you to your knees, so you can get even closer to your personal God. We talked and laughed and told stories, and when we were done, I returned to my room feeling uplifted and joyful.

The next day, I was invited to join Ram Dass at a party and *luau* some friends of his were having at their home on another part of the island. After his assistant Muid helped him into the car, Dassima got behind the driver's wheel and we were off. All three of us sang along to a Beatles' CD as we rode off to the *luau*. How surreal! I mean, here I was, in a car with Dassima and Ram Dass, all of us singing "All You Need Is Love!"

When we arrived at the *luau*, many people wanted to greet and meet and talk with Ram Dass. Because I was a guest at his home for more than a week, I felt no need to hog his time, so I strolled up a small incline on the lawn to watch the festivities. Ram Dass was instantly surrounded by people bowing at his feet, hugging him, and kissing his hands—strange behavior for Westerners, but very common in places like India, where gurus are revered. I watched with amazement at this very Western man being treated like an Indian guru, showered with adoration, love, and devotion.

Richard Alpert (his birth name) came from a wealthy family in Massachusetts. He worked as a professor of psychology at Harvard University before he and Timothy Leary were fired in the 1960s for doing experimental research with psilocybin and LSD, involving graduate students. After his own mind-altering experiences of heightened consciousness and transcendence using hallucinogens, he had traveled to India, met his guru, Neem Karoli Babaji (also known as "Maharaj-ji"), had his own spiritual awakening, and received a new name from his guru: Ram Dass, which means "servant of God" (in the Hindu religion, Ram or Lord Rama refers to an incarnation of god), before returning to the United States. He spent the next sixty years teaching about *love*—the embodiment of his guru's teachings. In 1971, he published the international bestseller *Be Here Now,* offering a map of spiritual reality still little known in the West at that time. From the 1960s till today, Ram Dass remains a leading spiritual teacher, bridging Eastern and Western wisdom.

As I sat on that little hill, I was struck by how his life, devoted all these years to spreading the message of *love* is itself so filled with love. Here he was in Hawaii, surrounded by a devoted staff of caregivers, people bowing at his feet, eager to pour their love and devotion into him. The thought "love begets love" echoed in my mind and moved me to tears. While I enjoyed watching the spectacle below me, I felt a confusing pang of jealousy. I had wanted a talk show all those many years ago as a platform to speak about love. I had spent twenty-five years teaching and leading workshops and seminars on love all around the world, but somehow I had not become the voice of love on the world stage I had imagined and even hoped for. A twinge of melancholy and envy coursed through me as I sat and watched the *luau* celebrants bowing to Ram Dass.

The next day when we met to talk, I shared this experience with him. I told him I was uncertain how I should be with him. He wasn't exactly my guru, yet I deeply valued his spiritual teachings. I didn't know whether to be with him as disciple-to-guru, student-to-teacher, or peer-to-peer. He replied emphatically: "peer to peer!"

He talked about how "Ram Dass" the spiritual teacher is a role, just like any other role; that we are just two human beings or, rather, two souls—or, more likely, one soul—occupying two bodies. I was struck by the complete and absolute absence of hubris and pretense of this man. Throughout more than thirty years of spiritual exploration and study, I have been around a vast number of spiritual teachers, leaders, and gurus. Rarely had I been in the presence of one who was so completely congruent with his or her teachings. Here he was, an eighty-one-year-old man revered worldwide for more than sixty years as a spiritual teacher, who had hung out with celebrities, spiritual leaders, and politicians . . . now here we were, sitting together in his home, and he welcomed me as his peer. I felt honored.

I showed him the film I had made on the topic of "Love," and read for him some of my spiritual writings. We talked and laughed and shared some more stories about our lives, and at some point, we lapsed into that same wordless, silent communion I had experienced with Stephen, the man I had met just after my marriage had ended. Only this time, the intimacy wasn't sexual. We sat like that, in a state of wordless soul embrace for what must have been an hour or more. Eventually, he broke the silence: "I could die right now and be completely satisfied." I burst out crying. His response: "You are spectacular!"

All my life, I had hungered for this quality of spiritual connection. In that wordless communion, I felt as though he had penetrated into my core, witnessed me there, seen me there, and honored me there. He had done for me what my father had never been able to do: He had seen into the depths of my soul, and genuinely honored me. Over the rest of my ten-day visit, we met regularly in his home, and most of the time we simply lapsed into that blissful state of soul communion during which he would inevitably blurt out something like, "You are sensational! You are incredible! You are spectacular!" On my last day, as we hugged goodbye, I said, "No matter what may happen in the rest of my life, I will forever be grateful for the time we've spent together."

"Me, too," he smiled.

I returned from Maui and my time with Ram Dass feeling an overwhelming sense of peace and well-being. I feel blessed to report that 2013 has been a calm and drama-free year after the upheavals of 2012. The medicine of having been *seen* and genuinely honored so deeply continues to nourish me like a time-release capsule, daily blessing my heart with its gifts of love.

I have finally integrated and internalized that "affirming masculine" in my psyche. Rather than hearing my father's voice inside my head—plaguing me with denigrating and demeaning comments and stirring up negative beliefs about myself—I have finally become my own affirming and loving Beloved. While most of my life I have longed for, and searched for, and ached for, an outer Beloved man who would finally see me, get me, affirm me, love me, cherish me, and adore me, I have finally become the one to see, get, affirm, love, cherish, and adore myself.

Many cultures and religions around the world speak about this "inner marriage"—the eventual integration of feminine (*yin*) and masculine (*yang*) within the individual. This inner marriage is regarded as a culminating and holy union within a person's psyche, heralding a new consciousness of wholeness.

We all know the moment of biological creation occurs when a sperm penetrates the egg and new life comes into being. Beyond this biological mystery, an even deeper, unfathomable, mystery confronts us: After years, lifetimes perhaps, of wanting and waiting, the creative life force finally penetrates and "seeds" the fluids of our longing—a holy communion initiating a divine pregnancy, followed by a divine birth. In spiritual terms, the god Shiva penetrates and merges with the waiting goddess Shakti inside the center of one's own heart.

Some days, I long for communion with another that fills me with a barely tolerable exquisite agony. On other days, the longing transmutes into an experience of Shiva making love to Shakti—all within me. And on those days, my bliss exceeds description.

Epilogue

The following captures Ramakrishna's first awakening to this inner marriage: "This is very secret talk. I saw a boy of twenty-three exactly like me, going up the subtle channel, erotically playing with the vagina-shaped lotuses with his tongue! First the anus, then the phallus, then the navel, the four-petaled, the six-petaled, the ten-petaled—they were all drooping—now they became aroused! When he got to the heart—I remember it well—after he made love to it with his tongue, the drooping twelve-petaled lotus became aroused— and blossomed forth! After that, the sixteen-petaled lotus in the throat and the two-petaled lotus in the forehead [became aroused]. Finally, the thousand-petaled lotus blossomed forth! Ever since then I have been in this state." *(From Kripal's translation of Bengali manuscripts.)*

I often resisted, kicking and screaming, as I navigated this long, arduous, and circuitous road toward my own inner marriage. But as I sit here today, on the second anniversary of starting to write this book, about to turn fifty-two, I celebrate this holy union and can finally say: I have become "a woman unto myself."

He came to me, finally, the Lover I had longed for all my life.

And he held my face in his palms and told me I was beautiful.

*And he made love to my body, knowing and cherishing every
longing and desire.*

*He saw the depths of my soul and was bewildered
by my beauty.*

*He treasured every feeling I had, licked the tears from my face,
traced my lips with his fingers, and held me in the profound
comfort of his embrace.*

*He anointed me in oils, bathed me, combed my hair, and of-
fered his undying devotion and worship at my feet.*

He covered me in rose petals and vowed to love me forevermore.

*He told me he had been longing for me, with as much aching in
his soul as I had longed for him.*

*And here, right here in the center of my own heart,
I found him.
The last place I had thought to look.*

Postscript

STILL AT RAM DASS' house, I awoke with a start early in the morning of December 21, 2012—the date of the Mayan prophecy predicting the "end of the world." Around the world on that day, people had gathered to meditate on universal harmony and peace—for example, at the Great Pyramid in Egypt, at Chichenitza in Mexico, as well as at sacred sites in Hawaii, Brazil, Russia, and elsewhere. I had gone to bed the night before completely unafraid of the world ending, certain that the prophecy was a metaphor for an old consciousness dying and a new one about to be born.

At exactly 4:30 AM, I bolted upright. Lying in bed, aware of the millions gathered in meditation around the planet at that moment, I felt myself levitating off the bed, as if raised by the collective intentions expressed around the world. The pulse of millions of people gathered in meditation was palpable and my entire body pulsated along with them. Try as I might, I could not go back to sleep.

So, instead, I got up and decided to join the millions and began to meditate. Almost immediately, I received a clear instruction: "Now! Now is the time! Prepare yourself to spread your father's ashes." I had brought his remains with me to Hawaii, stored in a flask I had picked up during my travels in India. I had been waiting for the right time and, apparently, this was it. I showered and dressed, and prepared myself for the ritual.

Still dark outside, the first glimmers of light already lit the horizon. Flask in hand, I walked along the street toward the cliffs, as if pulled by a magnetic field. In my dream-like state, the beauty of the dawn overwhelmed me, and I wept. I felt both of my mothers, my father, and my grandparents calling me forward, beckoning me toward the cliffs. With tears rolling down my face, and a mind empty of all thoughts, I walked on, gathering flowers in the growing light. I picked up a palm frond, wet with rain from the night, and baptized my father's flask to help send him on his final journey.

At that exact moment, the sun burst over the cliffs across the inlet, presenting me with the most breathtaking sunrise I have ever seen. I could feel my ancestral lineage surrounding me as if they were the cliffs themselves. Embraced by such an unfathomable love, all I could do was drop to my knees in gratitude.

Through my tears, I experienced the absolute perfection of my life. I sensed an invisible presence that has always guided me. I *knew* how profoundly loved and held I am, have *always* been, and *always* will be.

The time was right: I stood, opened the flask, and allowed the warm winds to carry my father's ashes back into the bosom of his beloved Hawaii. I thanked him, thanked both of my moms, thanked my ancestors, thanked the sunrise and the sky, and watched as the ashes flew over the cliff and drifted down to the sea below. When I was done, I created an altar circle of rocks and blossoms around the flask, in a small nook against the cliff where I had been kneeling, and stood to leave.

Walking back down the road to Ram Dass' house, I lay down in the middle of the abandoned, small, residential road and stared up into the early morning sky trying to absorb what had just transpired. My heart was too full to contain in my chest—even the infinite sky above felt too small to hold the vastness of what I was feeling. I don't know how long I lay there, overcome with emotion, but I eventually got up when I heard the sound of an approaching car. Just as I reached the house, a full double rainbow appeared right in my path. My father had been returned to his final resting place, and I, it seemed, had been welcomed with open arms back into Life itself.

Healing comes
from a heartbroken place
where you've breathed out
everything you carried.
Stay There.
The next breath is God's love.

—Alfred K. LaMotte,
Wounded Bud: Poems for Meditation

Acknowledgements

IN MY "VILLAGE" of friends and family who have supported me throughout this journey, I want to thank, in particular, my "soul sisters"—those wise, loving, and devoted girlfriends to whom I turn in my hours of distress, and remind me who I am, who have faith in me when I lose my way, who show up in body, heart, and soul when I need them, and who love me unconditionally no matter what: Dr. Caprice Haverty, Lily Myers Kaplan, Patricia Britt, Jodi Gold, Deborah Morris, Helene Roos, Marcy Baskin, and Damyanthi Chauhan . . . I wouldn't want to carry on this journey without a single one of you.

To my ex-husband, Dr. Keith Merron, whose love and friendship sustained my life for the twenty-three years of our marriage. Thank you also for the immeasurable gifts of our two beautiful children.

To the two greatest loves of my life, my son Joshua Benjamin Benson-Merron, and my daughter Maya Grace Benson-Merron: I have not known a greater joy or privilege than being your mom and, "*I love you more.*"

To the mentors whose wisdom, guidance, and support cultivated my gifts, helped me to heal, and guided me home:

Donna Blethen, Gib Robinson, and Seymour Radin. And to Ram Dass, for the glorious ten days you welcomed me into your home; my time there will remain one of the greatest highlights of my life.

To the clients and students I have worked with over these many years. Your willingness to daily let me into the most tender, precious, and sacred parts of your lives remains a privilege I never take for granted. I thank you for that, always.

To Stephen . . . no words were needed then, and no words are needed now, other than to say, "thank you, always."

To my editor, Dr. Christian de Quincey. Without your immediate and unwavering belief in this book, it simply would not exist. I cannot adequately express the gratitude I feel for that. And to Reba Vanderpool for your pivotal role in introducing me to Christian—none of this would have been possible without you.

And last but not least, to my moms Jodi Kirk for birthing me into this world, and Geri Benson for loving me into this world—and to my father, Frank Benson, for being the greatest teacher I ever had. I love you.

---❧---

About the Author

TINA M. BENSON, M.A., is a modern-day soulwhisperer and transpersonal/Jungian-oriented spiritual teacher and life coach. With a Masters degree in counseling psychology from Lesley College Graduate School, she has more than 30 years experience, both in the United States and abroad, teaching, leading, and facilitating individuals, and couples, as well as large and small groups through consciousness explorations, chakra initiation/meditation retreats, couples and women's retreats, ecstatic dancing, Voice Dialogue, Enneagram, chanting, ritual, and travel to sacred sites around the world. She is the founder and creator of the SoulSpeaks Project, creator of the short documentary film, *What Matters Most,* and is also a non-denominational ordained minister, officiating at weddings, birth, death, and other life-passages and celebrations. Tina lives and practices in Marin County, California. Visit: www.soulwhisperer.com

CPSIA information can be obtained
at www.ICGtesting.com
Printed in the USA
FSHW011953280419
57663FS